THE SHADOW OF THE BROAD BRIM

The author of this book was born in Terre Haute, Indiana. His education was received at the Bradley Polytechnic Institute, William Jewell College, and—in post-graduate courses—Leland Stanford University and the University of Southern California. Grand Island College gave him the divinity doctorate in 1929. From 1919 to 1924 he was pastor of the First Baptist Church of Riverside, California; from 1924 to 1931, of the First Church of Phoenix, Arizona; and from 1931 to 1940, of the Hamilton Square Church, San Francisco. He has been a General Evangelist and Pulpit Supply since 1940. Doctor Day began his literary career when a high school student as a reporter for the *Terre Haute Gazette,* and in the years since he has continuously written for publication. His "Beside the Golden Gate" column in *The Baptist* has attracted much attention and been widely quoted.

"He was a stout man and wore a broad brim hat."
                                                    –Costermonger's memory.

So far as I can make out the genealogy, that "Job Spurgeon" was my great-grandfather's grandfather, and I sometimes feel the shadow of his broad brim come over my spirit. There is a sweet fitness in passing on of holy loyalty. . . I like to feel that I serve God "from my fathers."*–C. H. S.*

THE
SHADOW OF THE BROAD BRIM

The Life Story of Charles Haddon Spurgeon
Heir of the Puritans

By RICHARD ELLSWORTH DAY

CROWN PUBLICATIONS

POWELL, TN

The SHADOW of the BROAD BRIM

To

DEBORAH

WHO SEEMETH ALTOGETHER
SUCH ANOTHER AS
SUSANNAH

CONTENTS

CONTENTS

LIST OF ILLUSTRATIONS

PREFACE

My introduction to the life and ministry of Charles Haddon Spurgeon came very early in my ministry. While attending a pastors' retreat in the mountains of East Tennessee where Dr. Vance Havner was the speaker, I had the opportunity to take long walks with Dr. Havner. On one of those walks I asked Dr. Havner for advice concerning the ministry. His reply was to become a student of the Bible and to read the biographies of great Christians. The biography at the top of his list was *The Shadow of the Broad Brim*, the life of Charles Haddon Spurgeon, by Richard E. Day. In a matter of days I had secured a copy and was deeply into the life of Spurgeon. Just as Dr. Havner said, it was "like reading about the life of an apostle."

For years it has been difficult to find a copy of this book called by many the most wonderful account of Spurgeon's life. We are thrilled at Crown Publications to make this book available to a new generation of men and women who are followers of the Lord Jesus Christ.

Whether you have just discovered Spurgeon or you are thoroughly acquainted, *The Shadow of the Broad Brim* will stir you to a more devoted life to Christ.

Clarence Sexton
Founder and President of Crown College

Spurgeon as John Ploughman

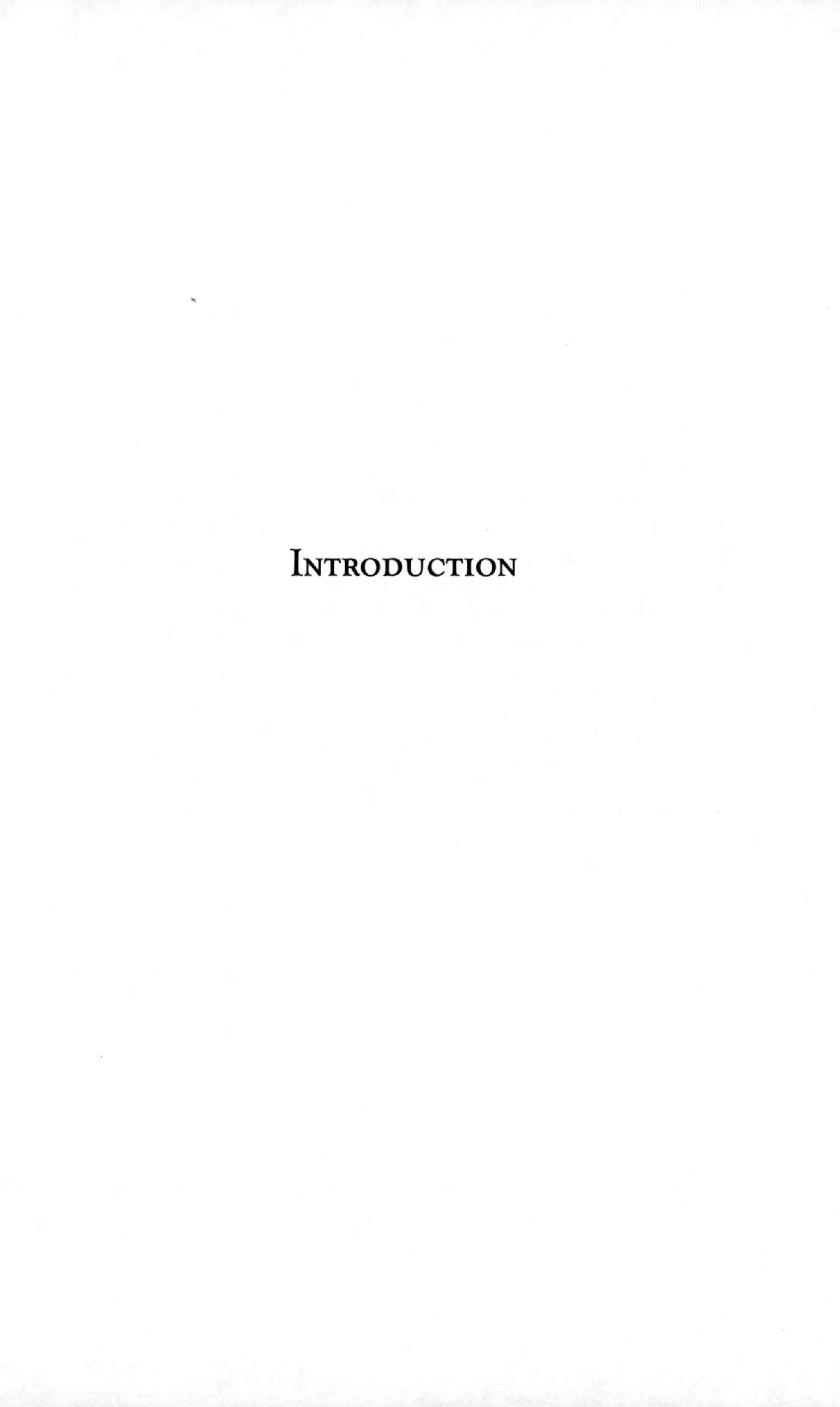

Introduction

The value of a biography depends far less upon its subject than upon its author. Milton mutilated by Ivimey, and Carey smothered by his nephew Eustace, are mournful instances of literary murder. James Hamilton has the singular good fortune to be embalmed by William Arnot, his own familiar friend and acquaintance, a spirit cast in the same fair mould, a genius wealthy in grace and wisdom. Apples of gold in baskets of silver are precious things in an appropriate setting, the golden apple being neither dishonoured by contact with a basket too homely, nor shamed by comparison with costlier metal than its own; the memorial of a good man's life should not be marred by poor writing: neither should it be overshadowed by excessive authorship.–*Spurgeon's Comment on Arnot's "Life of Dr. James Hamilton."*

Such biographical standards are too high for this humble effort. We prefer to adopt the scriptural formula–"We have this treasure in humble vessels of clay."

Introduction

Nearly all the standard Lives of Charles Haddon Spurgeon are out of print, and practically nothing about him can be obtained in the American book market. This in itself constitutes a worthy reason for a new biography.

Another reason is indicated by Garrett Putnam Serviss in his comment upon "The interest in human minds when the pendulum that ticks centuries moves back to the starting point." The nineteenth day of June, 1934, will mark the one-hundredth anniversary of the birth of Charles Haddon Spurgeon. The centenary of the birth of Henry Ward Beecher, June 24, 1913, proved an enriching event, not alone to the Congregationalists, but to the world. And the centenary year of Spurgeon's birth is sure to be a blessing to the whole church of Christ.

If any other reason is desired for this life, let it be the high value of biography in the literature of inspiration; especially the type of biography that rethinks yesterday's Great Hearts in contemporary language. The set, *American Statesmen*, was available for me in my early years, and read entirely through. The lives of George Washington, Alexander Hamilton, Thomas Benton and Gouverneur Morris left me in a state of spiritual élan for days together. It was at about this time that I heard Wayland Hoyt state that certain books, if carefully read–he named Fiske's *Critical Period*–would "make an epoch in one's life." This is highly true of biography. Spurgeon himself once said, "I always like to have a few good biographies handy, so that I can turn to the record of what the Lord has enabled his servants to do in the past."

Let it be quickly stated that when it comes to life stories none other has had such power over me as that of the Heir of the Puritans, Charles Haddon Spurgeon. Those great thoughts by which, as Fichte says, "men live," rush at one from Spurgeon's life as lions from a thicket. His youthful committal to the purpose of God is like a fire of reproof to those of us who still "endure the destruction that wasteth at noonday," and like "the shout of a king" to any modern youngster who ventures into a life of entire surrender to the will of God.

His contagious optimism that the Spirit will speak "awakening words" into the ears of the ministry of every age, and "that the conversion of the world need not go forward at snail's pace," will no doubt give confidence that the present century, strangely "confused with the near-wrongness of right and the near-rightness of wrong," is at the portals of a great awakening. His power as a gospeller who journeyed on familiar terms with the world of art, science and books of his day, yet made everything subordinate to the story of redemption, has a sharp surgical reproof for all of us who, in looking at Calvary, have allowed scholastic advantage to rob us of the fresh April wonder of a child. And, had I not long ago become a Christian, I could not have put a microscope upon the vast memorabilia of his works and letters, critically observing every movement of his inner-consciousness—I say had I not already been a Christian, his life would have broken me, and I should be ending this study on my knees, sobbing out, "My Lord and my God!"

Modern biography has a technique of its own, but no one has yet defined it. A well-known literary authority of San Francisco told me recently that there are no particular rules; "Just go to it!" In "going to it" I am keenly aware that research can dig up few new facts. Having become early in life a subject of large public interest, Spurgeon's biography was written to date each month in the forty years of his ministry. The mass and extent of this material is baffling. But—my own peculiar joy and task in writing this book is to recover the living charm of this little giant whose stature never exceeded "five foot six."

He has walked again in my study beside the Golden Gate. I have wept with him in his sorrows, and laughed with him through his Golden Days. Sometimes I have felt ashamed of my rude presumption in reading his love letters to Susannah Thompson Spurgeon; ashamed, but amazed at the crystal purity of their "Fellowship in Loveland with Christ." In all this research, and living through his days anew, a conviction has grown that Spurgeon's life will have untold value to our contemporary world; the story of this Mr. Great-heart whose life took on a peculiar radiance by reason of his adoring obedience to his Lovely Young Friend, the Carpenter of Nazareth.

Such an objective imposes its own rules upon the form of this book. Schweitzer is quite sure the *Living* Jesus has been lost by the biographers who have filled our shelves with books upon the *Historical* Jesus. So this book will omit much familiar material in the hope that, somehow, we may see this "Puritan bound in buckram" walk off the shelves of the nineteenth century, to be known afresh as he was in the days of the Tabernacle; a man who took life by the hand and romped with it; simple, humble, sincere; a fountain of good English after the style of John Bunyan; a person who, like Another, was a man of sorrows and acquainted with grief; a strange and irritating enigma to some who thought education creates genius; but an open secret to all who understood the hiding of power; a spiritual giant who moved across the fields of life battering down ancient strongholds with no other weapons than a blameless life and a boundless faith.

This type of biography demands chapters isolating for closer attention certain phases of his life; his sermon-craft, his personal evangelism, his debt to the Puritans, and so forth. The source-materials are all one could wish, with over 3,500 printed sermons; his priceless Puritan Library, now owned by William Jewell College, Liberty, Missouri; his *Letters*, selected by his son, Charles Spurgeon; the scores of books of which he is the author; the many biographies, some of which I secured only by wide advertising; and the nonpareil *Autobiography*, in four large volumes, prepared by Susannah and his private secretary.

Certain norms, therefore, grow out of the aims in producing this biography and shape it like invisible bell jars. I have seriously tried to make this a guided piece of writing, holding before myself and all of this age who may read, the glory of a Christ-centered life as the means of helping to restore "the lost radiance of the church," and the hastening of the full tide of another great awakening.

R. E. D.

I

Alva Scatters Dutch Fire

We were not aware that our little isle, the asylum of the banished, had received so great a reward for the entertainment of the Lord's exiles. England must have been a poor land until, in entertaining strangers, she entertained angels unawares. We are a very singular race; the Huguenot blood has had more to do with us than many suppose. Many of the Flemish, Dutch and French Protestants, driven by persecution out of their native country, found a haven of refuge in England. I remember speaking with a Christian brother who seemed right happy to tell me that he sprang of a family which came from Holland during the persecution of the Duke of Alva, and I felt a brotherhood with him *in claiming a like descent* from Protestant forefathers.–C. H. S.

Alva Scatters Dutch Fire

History offers a surprising detail for the beginning of this chronicle. Charles Haddon Spurgeon was not of Anglo-Saxon stock! His ancestors were probably Dutch refugees, who fled to England in 1568.

Biographers are in almost universal agreement on this point, save W. Y. Fullerton. He was very close to Spurgeon, and a leading man in the Pastors' College Society of Evangelists. To my mind Fullerton's Life[1] is the best written to date. Therein he says the theory of "Dutch origin has little to support it," and then gives astonishing support thereto by saying, "Many Dutch refugees settled in East Anglia . . . it is highly probable there was an appreciable mixture of Dutch blood in the family. Spurgeon was of conventional Dutch build, and there is a portrait of him and a portrait of Paul Krüger which very closely resemble each other!"

We hope that some European writer upon the Spurgeon Centennial will have the patience to glean out from old volumes and letters in forgotten libraries, even in Holland–as Chapman went to Spain for California history–certain details which even Spurgeon himself could never find. How fascinating should we be informed as to the very name of the clumsy little "Dutch Bottom" landing in the dead of night at a British seaport, among whose be-

[1] Williams and Norgate, London, 1920.

leaguered passengers were the Spurgeons. To be supplied with more data about the refugee family whose wooden shoes pounded upon the hospitable cobbles of Norfolk and Essex villages; yea, to track them back to the very farm or town in Holland from which they came, and to feel something of the zeal of their Protestant testimony.

For no portrait of Spurgeon is complete without the vivid background of the Reformation. It was from this flaming religious revolution in the sixteenth century that his forebears lighted their torches of spiritual liberty, and then passed them on to every child born in their homes for three hundred years. The scintillating radiance that shone in Metropolitan Tabernacle for over thirty years can be traced straight back along the fire-lines to "the greatest event in the history of civilization since paganism gave way to Christianity–the Reformation."

Stop long enough to consider this movement in broad brush strokes.

From the year 800 A. D., when Pope Leo III put a crown upon the head of the kneeling Caliban, Charlemagne, making him "King of the Romans," Western Europe passed under a papal despotism that interfered with every human and corporate relationship. At this remote date, one must spend long hours in careful research before sensing how heavily the iron hand of a degenerate church lay upon the face of life. Spurgeon himself felt that all of us ought to give some time to these pages of history in order, as he wrote, "that by God's grace enough of the characteristics of these good men (the Protestants) may be found among us to keep us from drifting utterly to Rome and perdition."

That ecclesiastical tyranny constituted the essence of Medievalism, the bitter flavor of which may be sampled in the remarks of a contemporary Vatican dignitary, "This fable of Christ has been to us a source of great gain."

Rome proved competent to put down with a heavy heel every protest for nearly a millennium, until the coming of Martin Luther, the monk of Wittenberg, in the sixteenth century. This youngster who had "inflamed his soul" by three years of meditation upon the Bible and the writings of Augustine, moved Germany as on the tides of the sea. "The Pope indeed! Who is he that he should forgive sins!" And when Johann Tetzel arrived in the streets of Jüterborg in 1517, headed by a cardinal's drum corps, prepared to set up the sale of pardons and indulgences to feed the extravagances of the papal court, the thirty-year-old Luther cried, "God willing, I'll beat a hole in his drum!"

Western Europe burst into flame-giving historians the complicated task of making separate accounts of the progress and persecutions that followed in each nation. Little Netherlands burned with marked brilliance. No other nation save Germany gave such valiant support to Luther's doctrines. These "Apostles in Wooden Shoes" registered a fresh Pentecost, lighting so brilliant a beacon that Philip of Spain felt himself goaded to stamp out Protestantism in the Low Countries: "I will not hesitate to rid my domain of heresy though a hundred thousand lives of my own should perish."

In 1567 Philip sent Ferdinand Alvarez de Toledo, Duke of Alva, to the Netherlands to fulfil this task. Alva was fully equipped. In his fifty-ninth year, a militarist from his youth, he embodied all the cold, cruel traditions of Spanish character. He commanded an army described as "one of the most perfect engines of war ever seen in any age." But his "killers" shed more blood than his conquistadors. He boasted when he left Holland that he executed eighteen thousand men. For this thorough work the Pope gave him a "Consecrated Hat and Sword as Defender of the Catholic Faith"!

But the "heresy" Alva went to stamp out, like burning firebrands, was simply scattered—even as an ancient record says, "They therefore that were scattered abroad went about preaching the word." England opened her gates to receive the hunted Protestants of the Continent; through those gates trooped Flemish, Hollandish and French refugees. They were a crusading company, regarding secular occupations as "simply their chief way of making a living, while Christian faith was their main concern."

Their coming was an unmixed blessing to England. Byles put the case in verse:

> And a store of wealth
> And a rich reward
> He brought in his open hand,
> For many a peaceful
> Art he taught,
> Instead of the fireman's brand.

These refugees brought their looms and skeins, starting at once to work "at the manufacture of sayes and bayes and other kinds of cloth, which met with a ready sale." Spurgeon remembered that in his early Essex days he still heard much of the "bay and say industry." He wrote from Mentone, while starting the autobiography that was never finished: "I dare say our fathers were poor weavers, but I would rather be descended from one who suffered for the faith than to have the blood of all the emperors in my veins."

However poor they may have been as weavers, these Spurgeons did excel in fervid witnessing for the faith. From the dense shadows that hide the early fortunes of the Dutch Spurgeons in England this fascinating gleam proceeds. There is in the San Francisco Public Library a large collection of the dry-as-dust volumes of the "Genealogical Philologist"; they show nearly a score of variants of the family name. One of them thus explains the origin of Spurgeon–"derived from the early Dutch 'spriggen,' referring to the language, and meaning 'eloquent'"!

II

The Apostolic Succession

One namesake, and perhaps an ancestor, Job Spurgeon, of Dedham, had to suffer both in purse and person, "for the testimony of a good conscience," as the Quaker record puts it. In 1677, a distress tax was levied upon him . . . because he had committed the atrocious crime of attending a Nonconformist meeting at Dedham! Six years later, he and three other godly men were recommitted to prison. This Essex Quaker was my great-grandfather's grandfather, *and I sometimes feel the shadow of his broad brim come over my spirit.* There is a sweet fitness in the passing on of holy loyalty from grandsire to father, and from father to son. I like to feel that I serve God "from my fathers."–C. H. S.

The Apostolic Succession

The several races of Protestant refugees who fled to England were swiftly fused into a new unity with the native stock, and in a far more powerful bond than blood or tradition—a glowing, spiritual fellowship that, as Johann Paul Friederich Richter said, was destined to "swing empires off their hinges." By the year 1575 a man's racial derivation had merely antiquarian interest; his spiritual kinship was the true touchstone. That sixteenth century in England was the original melting-pot, into which went Flemish, Dutch, French and British Christians, and out of which stepped—The Puritans! No one has ever so finely portrayed them in a few paragraphs as does Lord Macaulay in his essay on John Milton. Newell Dwight Hillis said of this characterization, "His words reverberate like thunder!"

It is to be hoped that the Spurgeon Centennial will attract the attention of the church to the "Puritans"—the richest body of divinity since Paul the tent-maker or Peter the fisherman. Spurgeon first came upon some of their books in a dark storage room of his grandfather's house when he was a boy of six. He was so stirred by them that during the next fifty years he ransacked England to secure their "rich racy writing," and dying left a priceless collection of them. He so lived their thoughts after them and was so shaped by their views that he became in the nineteenth century "The Prince of the Puritans," the heir and successor of their glory.

Great thinkers most often come singly; but sometimes in constellations like stars. This was strikingly true of the seventeenth century in England. John Bunyan (1628-1688) was not the only one whose words were bright and shining lights. He had a hundred worthy contemporaries; men like Owen, Charnock, Manton and Brooks. Nothing would so clarify the stream of contemporary English, and restore its early charm, as a reprint of these priceless old books; and nothing would more enrich the Christian message of this century than for the ministry of today to "take a long exposure" to the quaint and ravishingly beautiful truth-statements of the Puritan divines.

They were a dynamic race of men. Not being obliged to worry over some of the recent theories of education, they were accustomed to "bring up the babies on the body of truth," so that a child of twelve in a Puritan home could talk with intelligent skill on central New Testament doctrines. We are not surprised then to discover that their youngsters who "caddied for Manton" had a homiletical stance and swing at the very outset of their ministerial works which never can be gotten by a man who does not take up theology until he reaches the seminary.

These Puritans reared their children in the atmosphere of their own fiery convictions. They knew from babyhood the writings which were able to make them wise unto salvation, through faith which is in Jesus Christ. And those transforming correlates, such as "separation of church and state," and "the certain injury to the state upon the oppression of conscience," were the Puritan child's substitutes for Mickey Mouse.

The House of Spurgeon converged and swiftly united with the Puritan torrent. History gives only closely guarded glimpses of the Spurgeon fortunes, but such as we find are of a sort with the story of Bunyan.

There was Job Spurgeon of Dedham, who was a contemporary of John Bunyan. Spurgeon estimated that Job was his great-grandfather's grandfather. He was committed to the Chelsford jail in the bitterly cold winter of 1673 for the crime of attending a Nonconformist meeting. For fifteen weeks he and three others had nothing but straw bedding, Job himself sitting in a chair "the most part of the time, being too weak to lie down." Undoubtedly we have here a partial explanation of the terrible weakness that badgered Spurgeon's life, rheumatic gout, and brought him to an untimely end at fifty-seven. His grandfather James often said to him, "Charles, I have nothing to leave you but rheumatic gout; and I have left you a great deal of that." But without doubt we can here discern also the true line of apostolic succession: "I sometimes feel the shadow of his broad brim come over my spirit. I like to feel that I serve God 'from my fathers'!"

These Puritan Spurgeons through the twelve generations from their arrival, in 1568, to 1834, produced a sturdy race of Nonconformist ministers; of the Congregational order; stout Calvinists who steeped their children in the stern tenets of their faith. When the race came down to Charles, the very atmosphere he breathed in the home of his father John, who was a minister, and of his grandfather James, who also was a minister, was surcharged with all that related to New Testament faith, liberty of conscience and Puritan theology.

Spurgeon, though a child of the nineteenth century, was really a Puritan of the Puritans, the successor of a race of spiritual giants, and himself the heir and prince of them all. Once, while still under twenty, Spurgeon was engaged to preach at Haverhill, in Suffolk. There was a breakdown on the railway, so that he arrived at the meeting-house very late. But like sensible folks they had begun their worship, and when he neared the chapel he saw that his grandfather James was preaching. There he stood in his knee breeches, buckled shoes and frilly shirt, looking for the world like a Puritan picture from a Thanksgiving number of the *Saturday Evening Post*. When the old man saw Charles enter, he shouted, "Here comes my grandson. He may preach the gospel better than I can, but he cannot preach a better gospel; can you, Charles?" The young preacher said, "You can preach better than I can. Pray go on."

The old man wouldn't agree to that. Charles must take the sermon, going on with the subject just where grandfather left off. It was a circumstance seldom duplicated in the history of preaching. Several times the beloved grandsire pulled Charles' coat tail and "took a turn for five minutes." Spurgeon commented on this situation in a sentence whose significance he himself did not fully appreciate: *"Our agreement in the things of God made it easy for us to be joint preachers of the same discourse."*

After a while the old man no longer asked a turn, but sat behind Charles with his face aglow, saying in a gentle tone, "Good! Good!" Once he said, "Tell them that again, Charles!" Charles did tell them that again. In after years, when the old man had gone home to be with God, Spurgeon often seemed to hear the dear voice, 'long lost to earth,' saying, *"Tell them that again!"*

And Spurgeon commented simply on this beautiful memory: "I am not contradicting the testimony of the forefathers who are now with God. The doctrine which I preach is that of the Puritans: it is the doctrine of Calvin, the doctrine of Augustine, the doctrine of Paul, the doctrine of the Holy Ghost!"

III

The Unfeigned Faith in Thy Grandmother Lois

Children are their parents' heirs; the mercies of God are not the least part of the parents' treasure, nor the least of children's inheritance, being helps for their faith, matter for their praise, and spurs to their obedience." Our fathers have told us what work Thou didst in their days, in the days of old." Indeed, as children are their parents' heirs, so they become in justice liable to pay their parents' debts. The great debt of the saint at death is that which he owes God for His mercies. Therefore it is but reason that parent should tie his children to the payment thereof.*—William Gurnall (1617-1679).*

Schoolmasters are well enough, but godly fathers are, both by the order of nature and grace, the best instructors of their sons, nor can they delegate the sacred duty. When fathers are tongue-tied religiously, need they wonder if their children's hearts remain sin-tied? Religious conversation need not be dull!*—C. H. S.*

Charles Haddon Spurgeon was born June 19, 1834, in Kelveden, Essex, England. Which constitutes sufficient notice of Kelveden, for within ten months his parents Mr. and Mrs. John Spurgeon had moved to Colchester, and within eighteen months, "on account of unfavorable circumstances," the baby was sent to live with his grandparents, Rev. and Mrs. James Spurgeon, in the big old manse of the Independent Church at Stambourne. Here he remained for the next six years.

We may guess somewhat of those "unfavorable circumstances" when we remember that John Spurgeon and his tiny wife were but twenty-four and nineteen respectively when Charles arrived in the humble quarters of the quaint old Kelveden flat. Also, that baby fists tapped upon their doors with startling regularity in the next few years, until the family count stood at seventeen, nine of whom died in infancy, two boys and six girls surviving. In addition to this, John had ministerial ambitions, assuming shortly afterwards the pastorate of a small Independent church at Cranbrook. This he held for sixteen years, in a sort of itinerant ministry, which meant that he preached on Sunday at Cranbrook, and worked for his living (clerk in a coal yard) the rest of the week in Colchester.

The immensely valuable formative period of

Charles' life, therefore, was spent in the Stambourne manse of his grandparents, where abode also a maiden daughter, Ann Spurgeon. We might well take note of this family of three into which Charles came.

Rev. James Spurgeon, born in 1776, became pastor at Stambourne in 1810, and retained his post in high honor for fifty-four years, or until his death at eighty-eight in 1864. One of his contemporaries thus describes him: "He had a large head, and much good there was in it. He had also a large voice, and was very earnest, . . a man of the old school (Calvinism) . . . staid and uniform in his dress and habits. He wore the breeches, buckled shoes and silk stockings which marked the reign of George III, and he looked to be of a past age. He was the very picture of neatness, and resembled John Wesley. Was seldom without a package of sweets, which he gave to children wherever he went . . . was always happy in the company of young people . . . they attached themselves to him with a firmness after-years did not shake. . . Often desired he might speak of Christ on his dying bed, which was granted. He said (in those last moments) the gospel was his only hope; he was on the Eternal Rock, immutable as the throne of God. Those who did witness his departure from earth will never forget his joy and peace, and the glorious prospect he had in heaven." Let us hasten to say that even Goldsmith could draw no more charming picture of a parson.

And the grandmother was a worthy string for

the minister's bow. "Her piety and useful labors made her a valuable helpmeet to her husband in every good word and work." It was like looking upon Whistler's original of "Mother" to see her with an open Bible, sitting before the great fireplace, and to hear her quiet comments on the love of God. She, like her husband James, knew all the blessed gates into the city of child-soul: for each of those amiable wiles whereby grandmothers are presumed to spoil the babies she openly practised.

There was, for instance, the little shelf over the kneading trough. Thereupon, within reach of Charles' tiny fingers, she placed "bits of pastry, which, according to size, was a pig or a rabbit; which had little ears, and two currants for eyes; carefully placed in that sacred shrine like manna in the ark!"

One Sunday morning in the eventide of this worthy couple she remarked to her old husband that she did not feel well; would stay home, read her Bible and pray, while her Beloved preached. When the old man came back into the manse at noon, his heart broke to find her sitting in the old arm chair, near the fireplace, with her Bible spread out on her lap, her spectacles across it, her head bowed upon her breast-still in death. And her finger rested upon Job 19:21, "The hand of God hath touched me!"

There was also "Aunt Ann" Spurgeon, the unmarried daughter of the manse, the one child left remaining at home after seven others had departed and formed homes of their own. She was seventeen years of age when Charles came. This young girl was of a lovely spirit, with a positive reverence for the little boy, teaching him his letters, and storing up in memory, for hero-worship, every detail of his life. In certain of his days of great depression at Mentone, years later, Spurgeon remembered how her radiant young girlhood centered in him, and wrote, "How much they labored to spoil the child! Aunt Ann, who had a finger in it all, would spoil the child again if she had a chance."

These first six years of his life, from one to seven, stored Spurgeon's memory with gems which were his "diamonds among the rock crystals." Stambourne itself was one of those rural retreats not far from modern London—at least by auto; a crossroads village, where little farms converged. There was a blacksmith shop, a store in a dwelling, a cottage that also served as a school, and, quite near the cross-roads, the grounds of the lovely old manse and meeting-house. George C. Lorimer felt this countryside to be as "fair as paradise; verdure rich, soft, silken; flowers deep dyed; the lonely and oppressed might well court such sylvan solitudes and commune with them forever!"

The little village nestled at the very sources of the Colne River; within a few rods of the manse was the spring which formed its headwaters. A little farther down another brook joined the first and the Colne began. These little streams laughed and rippled through the sermon-master's utterances for nearly half a century. For hadn't he waded in them as a boy? And didn't he know that God never gave better music than their pebble-hindered waters? As far as lovely fern grots go—what excelled those nooks where mosses and evergreens laced their banks? Every factor was precious to his memory—the very iron weeds, rich russet in autumn; the far-spreading trees. The holy peace of these British streams got all mixed up in his soul with his dreams of the River of Life. And thus the glittering brooks of Stambourne kept singing in his sermons till his voice was stilled in death.

What a deep pathos years later to behold the stricken Spurgeon, on June 8, 1891, within a few months of his death, painfully limping through the streets of Stambourne with a photographer to see if any of the ancient glories remained. Well he might; for no child ever had his precious jewel casket of babyhood so packed with holy memories; those very early impressions that shape the rest of life.

The manse itself was described as a "gentleman's establishment," two-storied, mansard-roofed. There were certain dark rooms in it, made so by plastering up as many of the windows as possible, to escape the primitive window tax. In one of these forbidding chambers, the six-year-old boy found a copy of *Pilgrim's Progress*, illustrated with amazing woodcuts. He promptly carried it down-stairs to examine it in the mellow light of the big old front-hall fireplace. What a picture! No one could possibly call the baby boy who came down the great stair-case with Bunyan's book a handsome child—"very awkward, short, thick, heavy head of hair, mouth large, brown eyes with the mystery of dreams in them." When the lad put the book on the floor and lay flat to dream over the grotesque woodcuts, he felt so interested in the picture of Christian with a heavy burden on his back that, "I thought I would jump with joy, when after he had carried his load so long, he at last got rid of it!"

Spurgeon's entire literary style was powerfully shaped from this point on by John Bunyan. Before his death (to quote his own words) he read *Pilgrim's Progress* a hundred times. Here also, in this dark room, he found several heavy, immense books of Puritan divinity, and in tugging them down before the fireplace he launched himself upon a lifelong quest for Puritans.

The manse was a treasure-house for the lad, yielding for future use many "feathers for his arrows." There was the painting of David, the Philistines and Goliath over the fireplace; candle-snuffers, tinder-boxes, brimstone matches; a charming stair-case, a great clock, a dairy room; while outside, the grounds of the manse were beautiful with yew hedges, grass walks and emerald lawns. The pageants of nature were never forgotten—"The fragrance of the water which poured down in a thunder shower comes over me now."

Then there was in the same grounds with the manse the church-house itself, where Charles might sit Sundays beside his grandfather, before that worthy ascended the Jack-in-the-Box pulpit. There were lean-to stables beside the church where the worshippers could park their horses, naïvely bringing with them the long whips, to be set in corners of the pews.

At the end of six years "the unfavorable circumstances" in Colchester changed so that the nearly seven-year-old boy could return to his parents' home. But not without heartache. The elderly minister comforted his grandson on the night of departure by pointing to a full moon riding up the sky: "Laddie," he said, "we can both look on the same moon." And for years afterward Spurgeon's soul was strangely moved when he saw the moon, for he felt that somehow his eyes and those of his grandfather met there. And furthermore, their hearts were undoubtedly fixed upon the same celestial interests.

IV

And in Thy Mother Eunice

It is easy to observe that none are so gripple and hard-fisted as the childless; whereas those, who, for the maintenance of large families, are inured to frequent disbursements, find such experience of Divine providence in the faithful management of their affairs, as that they lay out with more cheerfulness what they receive. Their faith gives them ease in casting their burdens upon Him.–*Joseph Hall (1574-1656).*

I pity the wretch without a chair or bed on which to rest his weary limbs: but I pity far more the homeless creature who has no altar, no family prayer. The glory of Britain is her religion, and one of religion's choicest treasures is the Christian home. Who is so foolishly alarmed as ever to suppose that an invading host will ravage our fair shores when the whole land is studded with castles–not with turret towers, 'tis true, but yet with places where the God of Jacob dwells, residing as a fire around, a glory in the midst? –C.H.S.

And in Thy Mother Eunice

When the nineteenth century dawned the Puritan heirs of the Reformation had put aside their broad brims, silk stockings and buckled shoes; their women had turned British in bonnet and basque; but time had not woven a hair's breadth of difference between them and their forebears, the Halls, the Flavels and the Owens. At the age of seven, in the year 1841, Charles Spurgeon returned to his own home. His "bath of Puritan ideals continued without let." It was a home as deeply dyed in the oracles of God as John Bunyan's. Stop long enough to view this young family, these Puritans "gone Essex."

Spurgeon's father, John, was thirty-one, his mother, Eliza, twenty-six. The family circle had widened to include the baby faces of Eliza, James Archer and Emily. John had been born in the old Stambourne manse, July 15, 1811. A laconic contemporary record gives this description: "Portly looking man, good specimen of a country gentleman, and nearly six feet in height; did not fully enter on the ministry till he reached the prime of life; did good work, was much beloved; preaching-plain, earnest, pointed; manifested an affectionate solicitude for all under his pastoral care, especially young people." From the shorthand notes of Prof. J. D. Everett, made in 1849, we learn of certain great open-air meetings in Colchester, where the

Congregational pastor, Mr. Davids, preached; and that John, by the by, was selected to give out the hymns on account of the loudness of his voice, a quality which would appear to have run in the family.

Charles' letters to his father are fragrant with love, obedience and admiration; and in one there is an astonishing request for copies of his father's sermon skeletons—"they give me hints when a passage does not open at once." It was John's high privilege to observe his son's flaming career from beginning to end, and often to serve the lad as his earthly director and guide. His heart was completely filled with his son. At the laying of the corner-stone of the Metropolitan Tabernacle in 1859, John, not quite forty-eight years old, addressed his stentorian voice toward the Lord Mayor of London, who was standing in the speakers' group:

"My Lord Mayor, I am very happy to meet you tonight. We are Essex men. We come from Colchester. Colchester has something to boast of great men. I never had a headache in my life, friends, but if I ever had it, I would have today. This is one of the happiest days in my life. I feel beyond myself when I think of the kindness that has been shown my son when but a youth. I ascribe it all to God's goodness. I think, if there is one thing that would crown my happiness today, it would have been to see his grandfather here. He said, 'Boy, don't ask me to go. I am too old (eighty-five). I am overcome with God's goodness and mercy to me.' He is always talking about your pastor. Old people like to have something to talk about, so he always talks about his grandson." John Spurgeon died June 14, 1902, in his ninety-first year.

But we must hasten to affirm a mysterious physical law of the ages—great men bring the fires of genius from their mothers. All the world is debtor to the little known Eliza Jarvis, who is described as "a woman of marked character and devoted godliness." Grudgingly the yellowed documents of yesterday yield up, only after patient investigation, very meager details. Eliza was low in stature, plain, and of ample proportions—which accounted for Spurgeon's "five foot six and four foot three." She was a veritable Hannah in the manse, all the force of her Puritan spirituality flowing out toward Charles, her first-born. She was the mother of seventeen, nine of whom died in infancy.

Spurgeon wrote in after years: "I have not the powers of speech to set forth my valuation of the choice blessing which the Lord bestowed on me in making me the son of one who prayed for me and prayed with me. How can I ever forget when she bowed her knee, and with her arms about my neck, prayed, 'O, that my son might live before Thee!'"

If one seeks the power-hidings of the giant intellect of Spurgeon, the quest will end on finding a Puritan mother discussing with her children, from the time of their earliest memories, the great doctrines of Christianity. This gave Spurgeon very definite ideas as to religious education:

"It is said by some that children cannot understand the great mysteries of religion. We even know some Sunday school teachers who cautiously avoid mentioning the great doctrines of the gospel because they think the children are not ready to receive them.

"I bear witness children *can* understand the Scriptures. For I am sure that when but a child, I could have discussed many a knotty point of controversial theology. As soon as a child is capable of being lost, it is capable of being saved. It was the custom while we were yet little children, for mother to stay at home Sunday evenings . . . we sat around the table, and read verse by verse as she explained the Scriptures to us. After that was done, came the time of pleading; there was a little piece of Richard Alleine's *Alarm,* or Baxter's *Call to the Unconverted.* This was read with pointed observations to each of us."

One by one, each of her eight surviving children did ascend the bright stair-case of a mother's prayer unto eternal salvation. The itinerant preacher-father was much depressed one Sunday morning with fear and condemnation that he was neglecting his own bairns, while toiling for the good of others. With these accusing thoughts he turned back to his home. He was surprised to see none of the children in the hall. He relates:

"Going upstairs, I heard my wife's voice. She was engaged in prayer for her children: I heard her pray for them one by one, by name. She came to Charles, and specially prayed for him, for he was of high spirit and daring temper. I listened till she had ended her prayer, and I felt and said,

'Lord, I will go on with thy work. Thy children will be cared for.'"

This little mother in Israel died at the age of seventy-five, four years before her illustrious son. When the cabled tidings came from Mentone, January 31, 1892, of Spurgeon's death, his father, then eighty-one, bowed his head in grief, and finally said with choking voice, "What a happy meeting there has been between Charles and his mother!"

V

AND THE CHILD GREW

Children are in no case for enlarging possessions, heaping up riches, aspiring after dignity and honours; but merely take what is provided for them. The child, when it has lost the food nature provideth for it, is not solicitous, but wholly referreth itself to its mother, hangeth upon its mother. So for everything whatsoever should we depend upon God, refer ourselves to God, and expect all things from him.—*Thomas Manton (1620-1677)*.

Blessed are those circumstances which subdue our affections, which educate us into Christian manliness, which teach us to love God not merely when he comforts us, but even when he tries us. At last there must come an end to the nursing period; the boy ere long is quite content to find his nourishment at the table with his brothers. But he is weaned *on* his mother rather than *from* her.—*C. H. S.*

And the Child Grew

The eight and one-half years from August, 1841, to January, 1850, are of high importance in the life of Charles Haddon Spurgeon. Just as if his Young King were ordering his life in view of an early death, Spurgeon's character was "swiftly packed for the journey." His genius was of the type that rushes to maturity, so that by the time of his conversion, January 6, 1850, his mind had come to its ultimate set. Lodge, in his biography of George Washington, admits a sinister division in the soul of his subject even to so late an age as twenty-one; no one knew whether his powers would be unified or "go warring to destruction." Not so with Spurgeon. At the age of fifteen he had come through formative influences to a permanent disposition. His mind and soul became "a new, sharp threshing instrument," so amazingly efficient that biographers of the nineteenth century contended earnestly upon the question, whether the giant of middle life showed any marked improvement over the London boy preacher of twenty.

Convinced that neither ancestry nor environment can fully solve the equation of genius, we nevertheless view with fascination the swift strokes that helped make him during the critical years from seven to fifteen. For one thing, to quote H. L. Wayland, "he stored his mind with the colorful beauty of the fields and forests of England, whose rural scenes enriched his entire life and ministry." Of this we have already spoken. Forevermore, his sermons bore those pretty splashes of color that come only from memories of impressions that storm boy-soul. Who could have written the Twenty-third Psalm save one who as a mere shepherd lad was schooled in admiring God's pageants of glory? And what spirit could thus have brought June roses into London December save a man who as a boy loved the great out-of-doors? Listen to this sentence from Metropolitan pulpit—verily it hath morning dew upon it—"When this great universe lay in the mind of God like unborn forests in the acorn's cup."

There is the Knill incident. Much importance it had in Spurgeon's imagination, though it is not so impressive to a modern evidence-sifter. It appears that during this adolescent period, Charles spent his vacations for the most part at Stambourne, with his grandparents. In the summer of 1844, when Charles was ten, the Rev. Richard Knill visited James Spurgeon in the interests of the London Missionary Society. Knill was deeply impressed with the lad, and prophesied he would one day preach in Rowland Hill's Chapel. He also did a fine bit of life-changing with the child, early in the morning of three successive days, "praying with him in an arbor of yew trees, cut sugar loaf fashion." This was admirable, but the importance of the prophecy we are inclined to dismiss with the remark of a contemporary biographer, "Clergymen on a collecting tour are always much impressed by the high qualities of the children of the hosts."

Of greater moment was the incident of Spurgeon's first and last debt. This matrixed his amazing financial policies in all future ventures. When he was a very small boy, in pinafores (see *John Ploughman's Talks*), and at a woman's school (Mrs. Dearson's) he asked for a slate-pencil, on credit, from a kind dame shopkeeper, who handed it over—and he was in debt. He argued to himself that he would be sure to pay for it by Christmas with some fortuitous shilling. His father learned of the sorry business, at once—"some little bird or other whispered it to him, and he was down on him in right earnest." He gave Charles "a very powerful lecture" on debt; how it is like stealing; how a boy who would owe a farthing might one day owe a hundred pounds, get into prison, and disgrace his family.

Then he was marched off to the shop, like a deserter to the barracks, crying bitterly, dreadfully ashamed. The farthing was paid; solemn warnings; poor debtor set free like a bird out of a cage. And how sweet it felt to be out of debt! Years later when he was a great builder, developing his vast institutions, he persistently refused to "go any further than the funds." Once he wrote about it, "God bless my father! for what with companies, and schemes and paper money, the nation is getting to be as rotten as touch wood. Ever since I have hated debt as Luther hated the pope!"

Mention of the books he read during this period should not be omitted; they powerfully shaped his style and outlook. Mostly these books were old Puritans, the very ones that seem altogether passé to many contemporary religious leaders. Would that we could see on the shelves of today's youngsters books of the kind that molded Spurgeon: Baxter's *Call to the Unconverted;* Alleine's *Alarm to Sinners;* James' *Anxious Enquirer;* Fox' *Book of Martyrs;* Doddridge's *Rise and Progress of Religion in the Soul; Pilgrim's Progress*—of course; and even *Robinson Crusoe.*

Of outstanding importance was the resultant of forces that caused him to do a vast amount of memorizing during his salad days. His grandmother offered him a penny for each hymn of Doctor Watts' he could "permanently say." He found this method of making money so easy and pleasant that his grandmother first reduced the bonus to a half-penny, then to a farthing, to keep from being quite ruined in the deal. About this time his grandfather, plagued with rats in the manse, offered him a shilling a dozen for all he could kill. Spurgeon said: "I found rat-catching paid me better than learning hymns, but I know now which employment has been more permanently profitable."

The same astonishing application was followed by the boy in memorizing long passages from Bunyan's *Grace Abounding,* and reciting them, with great gusto, to his young companions. With what after result? No matter what subject Spurgeon preached upon in later years, he could with telling effect instantly recite a verse of a rousing Puritan hymn, or summon to his aid a passage of a stirring Puritan divinity.

Let us look for a moment at his school days. When he returned home at seven, his mental development was ahead of his years. His father placed him under the tutelage of a Mrs. Cook, wife of a sea-captain. Later he attended the school of a Mr. Henry Lewis; and toward the close of the period went with his brother to All Saints Agricultural College in Maidstone, where his uncle was a tutor.

In August, 1849, he was enrolled in the school of a noted instructor, Mr. John Swindell, of Newmarket. Here he began to work as an usher, or under-teacher, and made goodly progress in writing, reading, arithmetic, spelling, Greek and Latin grammar, and philosophy. It is well to be chary toward stories of unusual precocity in Spurgeon, but let us be assured that his mind had a robust excellence. His *Popery Unmasked*, written at fourteen, is unusual. In debate he often took both sides of the question, amusing and astonishing his auditors in hearing him refute his own arguments.

A full inventory of formative influences at the Newmarket school could not leave out Mary King, called "cook" by the boys; a towering, sturdy female servant in Swindell's household. She was a stout old Calvinist of deep religious feelings. When Spurgeon came under the agony of conviction in 1849 he sought her counsel. So powerfully did she impress her views that he later said, "Cook taught me theology." Like the Seventh Earl of Shaftesbury, his spiritual needs were supplied at this important juncture by a household servant. In the last three years of Mary King's life she was privately pensioned by Spurgeon at five shillings a week–belated, but timely tuition for a tutor in the School of Grace!

Spurgeon was converted in January, 1850, of which more detail is given in the next chapter. "Cook" remained close to the lad, pouring into his boyish soul her own sturdy Nonconformist views. On June 17, 1850, within two days of his sixteenth birthday, he quitted Newmarket, going first to Cambridge; "born again," his mind and soul stocked with priceless treasures.

The *Little Secret Diary* which he gave to Susannah shortly after their marriage had this entry, a tribute to "Cook's Calvinism":

> "*June 17.* Left Newmarket at six. Reached Stambourne at twelve. I had journeying mercies today. What can I write equal to the theme of sovereign grace? It is a miracle, a perfect miracle, that God should so love a man as to die for him, and to choose him before the foundation of the world."

VI

Pilgrim Loses His Burden

My soul was oppressed with horror and darkness. But God graciously relieved my spirit by a powerful application of Psalm 130:4, "There is forgiveness with thee, that thou mayest be feared," from which I received special instruction, peace and comfort in drawing near to God through the Mediator; and *I preached thereupon immediately after my recovery.—John Owen (1616-1683).*

I was once preaching, and I felt it was but dry work; but on a sudden, the thought crossed my mind, "Why, you are a poor, lost sinner yourself; tell it, tell it as you received it!" Why, then, my eyes began to be fountains of tears; those hearers who had nodded their heads began to brighten up, because they were hearing something which the speaker himself felt, and which they recognized as being true to him if it was not true to them.—C. H. S.

Pilgrim Loses His Burden

We are immediately faced in this chapter with some critical difficulties indicated by Hugh Redwood's *God in the Shadows*; namely, an intelligible analysis of a spiritual experience, the description of which employed a definite terminology one hundred years ago, but employs a very different terminology today. Strange new words, startling and sometimes alarming, are used by many to set forth the transforming of motivation, which in Spurgeon's time was called conversion and regeneration. Those, however, who have been sufficiently unbiased to look into this modern spiritual terminology are delighted to note a surprisingly familiar content; the same lovely treasure, unharmed, and for the most part "pure olive oil, beaten for light."

In this confusion of terminology, John Bunyan furnishes the least common denominator for everyone in explaining the reconstructive crisis. His Pilgrim was merely a wistful, defeated fellow, a stumbler after good, until that fair day when he was found running the highway with great difficulty, because of the load on his back.

> "He ran thus till he came at a place somewhat ascending, and upon that place stood a Cross, and a little below in the bottom, a Sepulchre. So I saw in my dream, that just as Christian came up with the Cross, his burden loosed

from off his shoulders, and fell from off his back; and began to tumble, and so continued to do, till it came to the mouth of the Sepulchre, where it fell in, and I saw it no more.

"Then was Christian glad and lightsome, and said with a merry heart, He hath given me rest by his sorrow, and life by his death. Then he stood still awhile to look and wonder; for it was very surprising to him, that the sight of the Cross should thus ease him of his burden. He looked therefore, and looked again, even until the springs that were in his head sent the waters down his cheeks. Now as he stood looking and weeping, behold three Shining Ones came to him and saluted him with 'Peace be to thee.' So the first said to him, 'Thy sins be forgiven'; the second stripped him of his rags, and clothed him with a change of raiment; the third also set a mark on his forehead, and gave him a scroll with a seal on it, which he bid him look on as he ran, and that he should give it in at the Celestial Gate."

That transforming experience came to Spurgeon at the age of fifteen, on the wintry Sunday morning of January 6, 1850. It followed a period of mental and spiritual anguish which began when he was a little over ten—five years in all. To Spurgeon the entire affair was the most important event of his life, and as such it demands a really guided analysis. Let us hasten to say that the restoration of the lost radiance of the church depends upon a thorough-going rethinking, yea reliving of the truth herein involved.

The final and acute form of spiritual distress rushed in full flood over this lad of the manse in the summer of his fourteenth year, while he was still in Newmarket, and it ran violently for nearly six months. He became faint, overcome with dread, full of penitence of heart, by reason of two related ideas: "God's majesty, and, my sinfulness." This laid him for weeks together in prostration of spirit. One who reads Spurgeon's full account is impressed that there never was a more poignant portrayal of what is called "being under conviction." Seeking for pardon; finding it not. Horror at the very memory of his unanswered prayers. Crushing sense of unworthiness. Lively consciousness of divine justice–resulting in the "choking of all utterance."

One might marvel greatly why this lad should have been taken for granted by his own ministerial father, and his deep needs allowed to fester. He could have been much helped by a wise soul-surgeon. Yet, nevertheless, this experience is generally a painful, lonely affair, utterly basic to effective Christian faith.

Spurgeon said, "Neither in the Church militant, nor in the host triumphant is there one who received a new heart, and was reclaimed from sin, without a wound from Jesus." He felt the necessity of his own goodness' being viewed as but a morning cloud and the early dew, and that it is to our blessed advantage that we see every tender bud of hope withered by our own lust. All of which constituted a set of "separate woundings contributing towards that killing by the law which proves to be the effectual work of God."

"I do not hesitate to say that those who examined my *life* would not have seen any extraordinary sin, yet as I looked upon *myself* (I saw) outrageous sin against God. I was not like other boys, untruthful, dishonest, swearing and so on. But of a sudden, I met Moses carrying the law . . . God's Ten Words . . . and as I read them, they all seemed to join in condemning me in the sight of the thrice holy Jehovah." No finer contribution could be made to contemporary Christian thinking than the complete publication, in book form, of that, the gripping personal account of Spurgeon's anguish over sin and joy in salvation. It could be entitled "For Sinners Only," and Russell's volume made a humble footnote.

In dreadful anguish, running with his burden, this young Puritan of the nineteenth century continues: "If I opened my mouth, I spoke amiss. If I sat still, there was sin in my silence. I was in custody of the Law. I dared not plunge into grosser vices: I sinned enough without acting like that. My impression is that this is the history of *all the people of God, more or less!* . . in this state, the Bible threatenings are all printed in capitals, and the promises in such small type we cannot make them out."

During this dark state of mind the lad went questing through all the churches in Colchester, seeking gospel light. None did he find, and none of the preachers helped him. One reason for this failure was that he still stubbornly held on to self-sufficiency, instead of, to use the mystic Puritan language, "hiding in the wounds of Jesus." Peace came to him at last, but only when "God gave me the effectual blow, and I was obliged to submit to that irresistible effort of His grace."

His final submission to irresistible grace came on this wise. The Lord's Day morning of the sixth of January, 1850, found Merry England in the grip of a driving post-holiday snow-storm. Spurgeon was bound for a certain Colchester church recommended by his mother, but the fury of the storm compelled him to turn down a side street. There he entered a tiny structure with the sign "Artillery Street Primitive Methodist Church."

Fifteen people, or less, made the congregation. Even the minister was snowed-up and didn't appear. At length a very thin-looking man, a shoemaker or tailor, agreed to do "the pulpit pinch-hitting," taking for his text Isaiah 45:22, "Look unto me, and be ye saved, all the ends of the earth."

The earnest but ignorant substitute spun the text along for ten minutes, emphasizing the idea of looking to Christ for salvation. Then he "swiftly came up short on the end of his tether." The sight of the distressed face of the boy, seated under the balcony, gave him "new leash." Fixing his eyes upon Charles and pointing with a long bony finger, as only a Primitive Methodist would do, he shouted,

"Young Man, you're in trouble! Look to Jesus Christ! Look! Look! Look!"

And Spurgeon did look—that primal act of faith whereby God gets his seal on the soul.

"The cloud was gone, the darkness rolled away, and in that moment I saw the sun! Oh, I did 'Look'! I could almost have looked my eyes away! I felt like Pilgrim when the burden of guilt which he had born so long was forever rolled from my shoulders. I could now understand what John Bunyan meant, when he declared he wanted to tell all the crows on the plowed land about his conversion!"

We cannot do better than allow Spurgeon himself to indicate the value of this "experience of Jesus."

"Precious is that wine which is pressed in the wine vat of conviction: pure is that gold which is dug from the mines of repentance: and bright are those pearls which are found in the caverns of deep distress. A spiritual experience that is thoroughly flavored with a deep and bitter sense of sin is of great value to him that hath it. He who has stood before God, convicted and condemned with the rope about his neck is the man to weep with joy when he is pardoned, and to live to the honor of the Redeemer by whose blood he is cleansed.

"I could realize then the language of Rutherford when, being full of the love of Christ, in the dungeon of Aberdeen, he said, 'O my Lord, if there were a broad hell betwixt me and Thee, if I could not get at Thee except by wading through it, I would not think twice, but I would go through it all, if I might but embrace Thee, and call Thee mine!'

"I now think I am bound never to preach a sermon without preaching to sinners. I do think that a minister who can preach a sermon without addressing sinners, does not know how to preach."

VII

Pilgrim Armed

The next day they took him and had him into the armoury, where they showed him all manner of furniture, which their Lord had provided for pilgrims, as sword, shield, helmet, breastplate, all-prayer, and shoes that would not wear out. And there was here enough of this to harness out as many men for the service of their Lord as there be stars in the heaven for multitude.

They showed him some of the engines with which some of his servants had done wonderful things. They showed him many excellent things with which Christian was much delighted. This done, they went to their rest again.

On the morrow he got up to go forwards. . . . But first, said they, let us go into the armoury. So they did; and when he came there, they harnessed him from head to foot, with what was of proof. Then he began to go forward, but Discretion, Pity, Charity and Prudence would accompany him down to the foot of the hill.—*Bunyan, "Pilgrim's Progress."*

Full and final decision to enter the ministry stormed the soul of Spurgeon the very day of his conversion. I have searched everywhere to secure the details of this radiant experience. He himself never saw fit to give them. Perhaps this was one of those things included when he wrote, "There is many a secret between us and our dear Lord. There are love-passages between Christ and the soul, which never must be told unless it be in choice company, and on rare occasions."

I have not had the courage to capture this mystery in a lovely summer gossamer of pure imagination; much regret that Guidance doth not permit. Particularly so, when one feasts his soul upon the double experience of Charles Grandison Finney: agony of heart in a rail-fence corner, in the Indian summer glory of a New England forest; followed by a seventh heaven in his law office; the taking down of his viol to sing of the Redeemer; the sudden flow of tears so that he was obliged to desist; the "vision of the Lord, face to face, and the baptism of the Holy Spirit"; and then, next day, the startled client who was told to get another attorney; Finney was now a retainer of the Young King! Spurgeon's must have been like that: and the narration of Finney's is the closest semblance Guidance permits.

Russell H. Conwell, however, gives the nearest

witness *after* the stone was rolled away: "The very next day found him visiting the poor and talking to his classmates concerning their religious life; and heard him declare to his teacher, Mr. Swindell, 'It's all settled; I must preach the gospel of Christ.' Notwithstanding his previous unimpeachable character, all his friends and acquaintances *recognized the great transformation.*"

We are constrained to discount as pretty, but irrelevant, the story of the ten-year-old Spurgeon's hay-rack sermons to his sisters, straw-pewed on the barn floor, with brother James in the manger as church clerk. We are sure it would have been a stage-coach drama had father John been a coachman instead of a clergyman.

We can dismiss with courteous brevity the story of his uniting with the Baptist denomination, its detailed account providing no particular timber for this framing. Conviction seized him as he began to read his Bible day and night, after January 6, 1850, that having believed, he should be immersed. A firm conclusion was reached within three weeks.

"From the Scriptures is it not apparent that, immediately upon receiving the Lord Jesus, it is a part of duty to openly profess Him? I firmly believe and consider that baptism is the command of Christ, and shall not feel quite comfortable if I do not receive it." (Letter to father, January 30, 1850.) "Conscience has convinced me that it is a duty to be buried with Christ in baptism, although I am sure it constitutes no part of salvation." (Letter to mother, February 19, 1850.)

"As Mr. Cantlow's baptizing season will come around this month, I have humbly to beg your consent, as I will not act against your will . . . I have no doubt of your permission. We are all one in Jesus Christ: *forms and ceremonies, I trust, will not make us divided.*" (Letter to father, April 6, 1850.) "If baptized, it will be in an open river; go in just as I am, with some others. . ." (Letter to mother, April 20,1850.)

And so it came to pass that Young Pilgrim went in "just as he was," on his mother's birthday, Sunday, May 3, 1850, and was baptized in the River Lark; as sweet a stream as was ever followed by the steps of Izaak Walton, and still dear to local anglers. The exact spot was Isleham Ferry, where the Lark narrows down, dividing Cambridgeshire from Suffolk; a quiet place half a mile from the village and rarely disturbed by boat traffic. It was one of Good Old England's cold May mornings, made yet more colorful–amid the signs of spring–by a cozy peat fire, ringed with white ashes, around which the people talked as they awaited the exercises. Spurgeon says he "was up early to have a couple of hours for quiet prayer and dedication to God." Then he briskly walked eight miles cross country to reach the spot where he was to be baptized!

We have a precious little word cameo of the lad on that Sunday morning: "Rather small and delicate, pale but plump face, dark-brown eyes and hair, rather deficient in muscle, did not care for cricket or other games, bright, lively manner, and a never-failing flow of conversation."

He was baptized by Rev. W. W. Cantlow, a returned Baptist missionary from Jamaica and for thirty years thereafter pastor of the Isleham Baptist Church. Spurgeon went down into the river dressed in a jacket with a boy's turned-down collar. As he came up out of the water he felt he "had lost a thousand fears in that River Lark, and found that 'in keeping His commandments there is great reward.'"

His mother said later: "Charles, I have often prayed the Lord that you might be converted, but never asked him that you might be a Baptist." To which Charles replied that God had answered her prayer with his usual bounty and given her more than she asked!

Our Young Pilgrim swiftly harnessed himself with what was of proof in the next four years. From the bafflingly ample source materials, including even the biographies hastily written by famous clergymen, "Lives" scribbled out in 1892 to sell to the mourners at the funeral, many rough ashlars are quarried for this opus. These books give us a glimpse as to how this harnessing proceeded. One of our sources consists of quotations from a small clasped book, a mysterious diary of his life during the critically formative April 6 to June 20, 1850. Spurgeon gave this tiny book to his wife in 1856. She understood, and did not break its seals until four years after his death, in 1896. I would give a king's ransom to touch and to read its tiny secret pages. Where is it today?

During these Arabian Days of spiritual nurture in

which Spurgeon, as Paul, received the preparation for his apostolate, choice seed was bounteously sown in every fair field of his life. "There is no time for work like the first hours of the day, and no time for serving the Lord like the earliest days of youth" (C. H. S.). He began by spending his Sunday afternoons distributing tracts and visiting the poor. He gave his Sunday mornings—at this tender age of fifteen—to teaching a class of boys, "who made wheels of themselves twisting around." Robert Brown, a fishmonger, was superintendent. Spurgeon did not seem to think that teaching would interfere with his studies, but was of a notion that clear Christian thinking could never be divorced from humble Christian service: "I learned to tell stories by being obliged to tell them."

In those formative days he gave himself with utter abandon to study, and to the service of God. And he "high-lighted" it all with meditation; lonely walks; such solitude as the mystic Emerson felt to be essential to radiance in the City of Man-Soul.

No more romantic picture is to be found on memory's wall than that of this Young Galahad, out-bound or in-bound, on a five- to eight-mile walk, preaching the gospel in some farmer's kitchen, or some cottage or barn. Verily, it would have given Reynolds a congenial subject to portray this youngster gospel-questing, on dark nights, as honest British rains were falling; dressed in water-proof leggings, a mackintosh coat, a hat with water-proof covering; flashing a dark lantern to show the way across the fields.

He did it all in simple love for his King. But the King was able therein to bestow upon him "the engines of war." These reminiscent words of the mature Spurgeon sound like a Psalm of David:

"Lo, I had a happy school, in which by continual practice, I attained such a ready degree of speech . . . up early . . . praying and reading the Word . . . all day teaching or studying, and teaching the Word at night. But I can bear witness that I never learned so much or learned it so thoroughly, as when I used to tell out, simply and earnestly what I had first received into my own mind and heart."

VIII

The Student Pastor of Waterbeach

Pray for the mantle, girdle, and blessing of Elijah, for the love of John, and the zeal of Paul, to twine hearts together to draw souls to heaven; till the Beloved comes like a roe upon the mountain of spices; till the shadows flee away, and the Day-star arise in your hearts. *—Samuel Lee (1625-1711).*

I vow to glory alone in Jesus and His cross, and to spend my life in the extension of His cause, in whatsoever way He pleases. I desire to be sincere in this solemn profession, having but one object in view, and that to glorify God. Help me to honor Thee, and live the life of Christ on earth!*—Ministerial resolutions, from the "Little Secret Diary" of C. H. S., entry of May 3, 1850.*

The Student Pastor of Waterbeach

On the day after Spurgeon's sixteenth birthday arrangements were completed for his entry in the Cambridge School of E. S. Leedings, who had known him since his ninth year. It was "a matriculation in poverty," through which Jehovah adds a sweet flavor to the training of his prophets. What a multitude of us feel a lump in our throats at the very recollection of student days; threadbare garments, barren rooms, lonely hours, and poignant memories of small money sums from impoverished parents. That money now seems as holy to us as the waters of Bethlehem to David. Let us hasten to record Spurgeon's sharing in the bitter-sweet truth that the King has no fairer way to constrain his chosen than in the tear-stained memory of an education had at the blood-sacrifice of a devoted father and mother. Should it not, therefore, be poured out unto Jehovah?

Thus he became for three years a Cambridge man, though he never entered the university. His expenses were met in part through work as an under-teacher; in 1853, he advertised he would privately tutor several pupils in mathematics, grammar, drawing and history, at a tuition of $25 per year. This he never did. His formal education abruptly ended in the summer of 1853 by his removal to Waterbeach.

His call to the ministry was highly prized by him, and as Martin Luther said, "did much inflame his heart." In a letter to his father, 1850, he wrote: "How I long for the time when it may please God to make me, like you, my father, a successful preacher of the gospel. Oh that I might see one sinner constrained to come to Jesus! I almost envy you your exalted privilege."

Arriving in Cambridge, he immediately united with the St. Andrews Baptist Chapel, chiefly because that church sponsored an organization called "The Lay Preachers' Association." Despite his tender years, he was immediately voted into the Preachers' Association. This created the occasion of his first sermon, in the fall of 1850. The vigorous old president of the Association, Rev. James Vinter, assigned him and another lad to take charge of a Sunday evening service in a Taversham cottage, four miles away. Each thought the other was to do the preaching. Disillusionment came during the walk to Taversham, when Spurgeon wished God's blessing on his friend's sermon. The other boy said, "Never! I was asked to walk with you, and I hope God will bless *you* in *your* sermon!" Spurgeon said, "My inmost being was all in a trouble!"

When the two lads entered the low room of the thatched cottage they found there a few farm laborers and their wives. Spurgeon was attired in a round jacket and a broad turn-down collar. He "got his text on his feet," 1 Peter 2:7, "Unto you therefore which believe he is precious." To his delight he did not break down, was not destitute of ideas, and did not stop short in the middle. Nevertheless, he was glad to see the way to a fair conclusion, and give out a hymn. His extreme youth was a marvel to the cottagers. "Bless you, dear heart, how old are you?" questioned one elderly woman. "Under sixty. Never mind my age; think of Jesus," Spurgeon replied. He promised to come again if the gentleman at Cambridge thought him fit.

This brings us to the lovely chronicle of his first pastorate, a Baptist church in a place called Waterbeach, five miles from Cambridge. The church edifice was small, originally a barn, walled of adobe, plastered within and without, surmounted by a thatched, steep-pitched hip-roof. The assembly-room was seated with rude benches, below a high pulpit. When empty "it did appear sterile and barren, but seemed like heaven with God's people in it." Waterbeach itself was a village in a rural world that preserved much of the religious sincerity of the Puritan era. The Lay Preachers' Association assigned him there, Sunday, October 12.

His sermon theme was "Salvation from Sin," and the text, Matthew 1:21. Less than twelve were present. They liked him well enough to ask him to preach the two succeeding Sundays. He walked over from Cambridge each time. This continued several months. They esteemed him, "a dear, good boy, on an evangelistic mission." A possible pastor? Unthinkable! Such men as Rowland Hill had served them. But the lad's influence widened so swiftly that early in 1852, Waterbeach issued him a formal call. He accepted, after many hours of prayer. The salary was fixed as $225 a year; insufficient to keep him, but the good people brought him bread, produce; and "always thought of him when they killed a pig." He paid twelve shillings a week for his quarters. Of course, he kept on walking, though "there was a rail there and back from Cambridge."

Thus at sixteen he began a pastorate of nearly two and a half years, from January, 1852, to May, 1854. It was a basic experience for him. He learned the rare art of handling hard cases–"perfectionists, half-and-halfers, hypocrits and misers." Uncouth bombast was neatly taken out of him by painfully frank country folk; and it should be said that Spurgeon could "take it." Good Deacon King, a miller with his cottage by the mill, loved the lad, but toned him down in the matter of unguarded pulpit utterance by such simple expedients as sticking a pin in Spurgeon's Bible at Titus 2:8. He gained the priceless grace of being at ease with common people, through living for a few days in practically every home of his flock. There were transforming friendships–such as that with Pastor Cornelius Elven of Bury St. Edmunds, who, after preaching Spurgeon's first Waterbeach anniversary sermon, said to him, "Lad, study hard; keep abreast your foremost Christians; for if they outstrip you in knowledge of Scripture, or power to edify, they will be dissatisfied with your ministry." "That spur was useful," Spurgeon commented.

From Waterbeach his evangelical passion dated, which, to quote Adkins, was "the schooling for his larger ministry and helped make that ministry possible." He immediately began a wide apostolate, preaching everywhere he was asked, many times each week, thus acquiring by doing the exquisite pulpit technique that brought the world to his doors.

But if Waterbeach shaped him, it should be said that he transformed Waterbeach. At the beginning of his work, moral conditions there were black; "drunkenness, debauchery, profanity, all mixed up with poverty." The lone-handed student pastor had such a seal from God that he forthwith changed the face of things. This pastorate might form another chapter in the radiant chronicle that Sylvester Home calls "The Romance of Preaching."

In a few weeks the little chapel was packed, "It pleased God to turn the whole place upside down." It was the ancient miracle of the Spirit honoring "a lad with a blameless life and a golden message." Those who used to do mischief were now in the house of God, rejoicing to hear of Jesus crucified, "listening their very hearts away to a voice that told of Christ weeping over forgotten men, reprobates, despisers, drunkards, and old men on the brink of hell; the lonely, the weary, the defeated."

Small wonder the membership climbed from forty to a hundred. The simple-hearted people of Waterbeach gave the bonnie lad their hearts without reserve. On the day that Spurgeon hinted the possibility of his going to London, this little Zion found "her tears were on her cheeks"; they sobbed, "Lord, keep him here!" Years later, an honest old deacon of Waterbeach made his first trip to London. They showed him the glories of the Metropolitan Tabernacle; but he had no eyes for that. On his return to the little thatched church, he was asked to tell what he had seen. Memory grew confused; his voice failed; but there was one lustrous experience that eclipsed all London: he could speak of that–"Mr. Spurgeon was very glad to see me."

IX

THE SUSTAINED SURRENDER

There are so many vices and imperfections in our nature, and we are so feeble and weak, that we have very great need daily to pray unto Him, yea, and that more and more, that He will not suffer us to decline from His will.—*John Calvin (1509-1564.).*

I would wail out my penitent confession of times in which I failed to observe unvarying allegiance to my Lord. I pray God, if I have a drop of blood in my body which is not His, let it bleed away.—*C. H. S.*

The Sustained Surrender

During the Waterbeach pastorate Spurgeon entered the second of those two transforming experiences that have together formed the pier-heads supporting Christian power in all generations since Pentecost—*a thorough surrender to the will of Christ, continuously sustained, in every area of life.* The other experience, of course, was his new birth. The two stand related to each other with the same integrality as Christ's death and resurrection. Each confirms the other and makes it valid.

We carefully skirt the borders of controversy in this book. Yet here is an area of practical Christian mysticism that challenges a fresh evaluation in an age whose Century of Progress is miraculous in the mechanical and stereotyped in the spiritual. Among the most romantic pages of Christian history are those that record the story of small groups of people who from time to time recover the lost radiance of the church, and by reason of their resistless spirit make conventional religion appear drab indeed. These New Testament holiness movements, often strangely different in terminology and disposition, have a vital unity in certain deep, hidden agreements, and are really convergent streams toward one great flood that shall some day cover the earth with the glory of God—brothers, under the skin, all the way from the Moravians to the Victorious Life Movement.

Every century since Pentecost has produced such dynamic sectors in the church. Upon anyone who will critically investigate this phenomenon, patience will confer her richest rewards. That person will discover, with amazement, that these movements emphasize eight principles, the chief of which is this: An original and thorough invasion of every area of personality by the will of Christ, daily sustained by fresh waiting upon him, resulting in a life completely disciplined to his will—clear out to the finger-tips.

Let no one imagine that Revision and Invasion very often enter man-soul together. They do not. In most cases, they are separated by a considerable space of time; earnest ministers of the gospel preaching ordinarily until on a sudden they find Pentecost. This is the story of Moody, who lighted his torch from Spurgeon's; of Savonarola and Fenelon—and what shall I say more? For time would fail me to speak of Fox and Bunyan, of Wesley and Whitefield, of Finney and Gordon, who by reason of a broken will entered into a blessed walk; subdued kingdoms, wrought righteousness, and effectively labored to win for the Lamb that was slain the reward of his suffering!

So far as Christian fruit-bearing goes, this pair of twin fountains, Revision and Invasion, thrusts genius and education into the background of ordinaries, and explains the paradox of uneducated ministers so often leading the church toward the Promised Land. In Christian labors, shoddy intellectual work and lack-luster witnessing are due in no case to a lack either of native genius or subsequent intellectual training, but *to a defective spiritual experience.* This is a hard fact for men who stake their futures on curricula, and then cover up their inner lack with a cheerful professional air. It also explains why Spurgeon did not appeal to certain men who saw in him naught but "a green London preacher."

Spurgeon's apostolic accolade came to him on this fashion. Friends and relatives alike agreed that the lad was of uncommon cut, and that therefore a thorough education ought to be had. Dr. Joseph Angus, of Stepney's College (now Regent's Park College), wrote to a Waterbeach deacon, "His usefulness will be very much greater with preparation than without it." Here is Spurgeon's characteristic reaction: "Although I hoped that I might be useful without a college training, I consented to the opinion of friends that I should be more useful with it: I have an aversion to college, but I must not consult myself, but Jesus."

An arrangement, accordingly, was made for him to meet Doctor Angus for conference on a certain morning in the Cambridge home of Mr. Macmillan, the publisher. Spurgeon was on time; so was Angus. But, the house being commodious, the stupid servant girl put the men into different rooms. Each waited till patience had her perfect work and then departed. Thus a strange providence put an end to Spurgeon's higher education.

There is no use in minimizing Spurgeon's bitter disappointment when he learned of this unhappy mistake. Occasional nettled sentences of pique are found scattered through his utterances in the after years. Speculation on might-have-beens is very painful, either extreme of opinion only making one feel sorrier. Doctor Conwell remarks, "Spurgeon would not have been the Elijah of his age with the usual college education." Yet one of Spurgeon's warmest admirers said: "With an education his sermonic literature would not have lost its fire, but would have found the literary immortality which it just missed." We leave the problem in the hands of God, urging alike the scholastic never to assume that education is a *sine qua, non*, and the young student never cheaply to cut intellectual corners, on Spurgeon's example. The rest of us must remember that with or without higher culture nothing but futility results from the lack of a primitive and sustained surrender to the will of Christ.

On the afternoon of this day of disappointment, Spurgeon walked alone with his sorrow over Midsummer Common, toward a little wooden bridge that used to be on the way to Chesterton. In the midst of the Common he heard "what seemed to be a loud voice, but may have been a singular delusion." At any rate, God made overtures to his soul in those unforgetable words from Jeremiah, "Seekest thou great things for thyself? seek them not!"

He was not disobedient. Years later we find him saying, "From that first day until now, I have acted on no other principle but that of perfect consecration to the work whereunto I am called. I surrendered myself to my Saviour, I gave him my body, my soul, my spirit . . . for eternity! I gave him my talents, my powers, my eyes, my ears . . . my whole manhood! *So far from regretting what I then did, I would fain renew my vows and make them over again!*" Disciplined to the finger-tips? Hear this: "If Christ commands me to hold up my little finger, and I do not obey him, it looks like coolness in my love to him."

And thus at the morning age of eighteen he stood ready for world service, his heart revised and invaded by the Son of God. "There was nothing in him necessitating delay! He could be placed in the seat of honor, for he had the spiritual grounding requisite. The light was there, it needed but a stand adequate to its power of illumination. He had foresworn the search of great things for himself, and what is this in the economy of grace, but the forerunner of promotion?"[1]

[1] *James Douglas, C. H. Spurgeon.*

Spurgeon at Twenty-one

This portrait was a lover's gift to one who was very soon to become his bride, and I recall how in the glamour of "love's young dream" I used to gaze on the sweet boyish face and think no angel could look half so lovely. Many a time, during my husband's long absences when fulfilling his almost ceaseless preaching engagements, has this portrait comforted me; its expression of calm, confident faith strengthened my heart, and I used to think the upraised finger pointed to the source whence I must draw my consolation.—Susannah Thompson Spurgeon.

X

LONDON FINDS HIM

Why are the clergy not only restless, but sometimes miserably unhappy, hopelessly fallen from early enthusiasms? *–Bishop Fiske.*

I would answer, that kind of a man is unsurrendered to God's will for his life. And when he surrenders himself, he surrenders his job and the geography of it!*–The Puritan of Gramercy Park.*

I remembered the poor but loving people to whom I ministered, and the souls which had been given me in my humble charge: and though I anticipated obscurity and poverty as a result, yet I did then and there renounce the offer of collegiate instruction, determining to remain preaching the Word so long as I had strength to do it.*–C. H. S.*

London Finds Him

Let us trace the providential circumstances that brought the surrendered lad to London. In the summer of 1853 he gave an address before the annual meeting of the Cambridge Sunday School Association in the Guildhall of the town. His extreme youth (nineteen) caused two of the subsequent speakers on the program publicly to make very personal and insulting observations. One asked why he left his sheep in the wilderness. The other remarked that it was a pity boys did not adopt the scriptural practice of tarrying at Jericho until their beards were grown, before trying to instruct their seniors. Young Spurgeon rose to his feet to rejoin that the individuals referred to in Scripture were *men*, not *boys*: the true application of the text being–in the case of ministers–to those who had fallen into sin, and needed seclusion until character had been to some extent restored. This was an accidental center shot, for his antagonist was just that kind of preacher.

But London found him that evening. In the audience was a young man, George Gould, a deacon of the Baptist Church of Loughton. He so admired the fine Damascus blade of the young dominie that when he returned to London he urged Thomas Olney, a deacon of New Park Street Baptist Chapel, to secure Spurgeon's services for their pulpit, then vacant: "If you want to fill your empty pews, send for a young man I heard in Cambridge, by the name of Spurgeon." A single recommendation was insufficient, Gould had twice to urge the matter upon Olney. The New Park Street Chapel was utterly discouraged with candidates—"They never asked one of them twice; such philosophical, or dry, or learned, sermons!—once was enough." But at last a letter was sent to Spurgeon inviting him to preach.

The New Park Street Chapel was one of the leading three of the hundred and thirteen Baptist churches of London: its church book shows a membership in January, 1855, of three hundred and thirteen. That was after Spurgeon had been pastor eight months; no accurate statistics are available as to the number when he began; Fullerton says two hundred and thirty-two. That number after two hundred years of history!

In those two centuries three notable preachers had served them: Benjamin Keach, of martyr fame, thirty-six years (1668-1704); ponderous John Gill, of the more ponderous *Commentary*, fifty-one years (1720-1771); John Rippon, of hymn-book fame, sixty-three years (1773-1836).

When the London Bridge was built in 1831 the church was worshiping in a chapel in Carter's Lane, and the edifice was in the way of the approach. It was sold out, and a cheap lot purchased in River Flood district—the gloomy, narrow streets of a dingy, repellent section of London. Here the parsimonious fathers built an edifice seating twelve hundred, the New Park Street Chapel, and sat down to wait for dry rot. It came. In 1854, the handful of the faithful gathered on Sunday like a huddle in an empty ocean of wood, "Ichabod" being written all over the place.

The letter of invitation was handed Spurgeon when he walked into the Waterbeach Chapel from Cambridge on Sunday morning, November 27, 1853. It grips one's heart with something like a high dramatic climax to behold him, completely emptied of self, read the letter, then hand it over to a deacon: "Must be a mistake; couldn't be for me; evidently meant for someone else with the same name." On Monday he sent a timid letter (I'd give a king's ransom to own it) delicately suggesting an error: *must* be an error; he was only nineteen years old, and nobody knew him out of Waterbeach. The return post from London read, "You're the one, no mistake." Thus it happened that he was dated to preach in London, December 18, 1853.

In a movie-minded age we hasten to say that nothing on the silver screen today has such heart-filling, tear-compelling interest as the mighty drama that followed. On Saturday afternoon, December 17, a lad alighted from the East Counties Railway at the Bank Station. Distinctly rural appearance; yea, verdant green, rivalling a Solomon lily; with a huge black silk stock and large blue silk kerchief, with eloquent white spots, protruding from his breast pocket. This he flourished, when preaching, with much effect, under the impression that it was the fashion in London. The deacons gave him a dozen white handkerchiefs a little later!

That Saturday night was marked by the "big-city blues." He lodged in a boarding-house in Queen Square, Bloomsbury, and got a thorough twitting from the young men who lived there. They told him about *really brilliant* preachers in London who for the most part had a hard time keeping their pews filled. Spurgeon retired, terribly depressed, to a narrow bed "in a cupboard over the front door." A scenarist would revel in his mental reactions that night:

"Pitiless was the grind of the cabs in the street, pitiless the recollection of the young city clerks, pitiless the spare room which scarcely afforded me space to kneel, pitiless even the gas-lamps which seemed to wink at me as they flickered amid the December darkness. I had no friend in all that city full of human beings, and to escape safely to the serene abodes of Cambridge and Waterbeach seemed Eden itself."

Sunday morning, December 18, dawned clear and cold. He walked over to the chapel through a dreary wildness of brick, and was further depressed by the imposing New Park Street structure, suggesting a wealthy and critical audience, far removed from the ministry of sweetness and light among humble folks at Waterbeach. Only one consolation rose up—the audience was likely to be small. It was—eighty persons!

He preached that morning on "The Father of Light," with James 1:17 as a text. Enough interest arose to cause the people to do much talking in the afternoon, so that the evening audience was larger than normal. He preached from Revelation 14:5, "Without fault before the throne." G. Holden Pike, with a historian's care, interviewed people who attended that service:

> "The effect was amazing; impossible to describe the emotions of the congregation; nearly all were at last raised from despondency; after the service people too excited to leave the building gathered in groups talking about securing him for pastor; deacons came out of the vestry and promised to use their endeavors to secure him. Dear old Unity Olney (wife of the deacon, Thomas), a semi-invalid, attended that night and when she got home said to her husband with deep emotion and peculiar emphasis, '*He* will do!'"

The history of final settlement as pastor may be swiftly set down. He made three more visits in January, 1854, and was then invited to occupy the pulpit six months on probation. He thought this too long, unfair to the church, and cut the time to three months—"The congregation might not want me, and I do not wish to be a hindrance."

But the congregation had other ideas. Fifty men of the New Park Street Church, by a peremptory signed requisition, demanded a special church meeting for April 19. At this session the church voted that they considered it "prudent to secure as early as possible his permanent settlement among us." The church issued him a call.

Spurgeon replied, April 28, "There is but one answer to so loving and candid an invitation. I accept it." The call not being quite unanimous, he added kindly words for the few who voted against him; he "respected their honesty, only wondered there were not more." And with surpassing humility he concluded, "Remember my youth and inexperience, and pray . . . forgive the mistakes I may make, or unguarded words I may utter." The salary agreement at the beginning was "pew rents"; his first year's income was less than $1,500.

Thus began "the flaming apostolate." He had lost his thousand fears of London after that first December evening service. "The Lord helped me graciously. When at night I trudged back to the Queen Square narrow lodging, I was not alone, and I no longer looked on Londoners as flinty-hearted barbarians. I wanted no pity from anyone, I did not care a penny for the young lodgers, nor for the grind of the cabs, nor for anything else under the sun. *The lion had been looked at all around, and his majesty did not appear to be a tenth as majestic as when I had only heard his roar miles away!*"

Spurgeon at Twenty-six
First Years of Ministry in the Tabernacle

XI

The World Goes to John

God does not prolong the lives of His people that they may pamper themselves with meat and drink, sleep as much as they please, and enjoy every temporal blessing; but to magnify Him.—*John Calvin.*

The Lord's prophets shall live on in the midst of famine, and war and plague till they have uttered the words of their prophesy; His priests shall stand at the altar unharmed while there is a testimony for God, and till their last sacrifice has been presented before Him.—C. H. S.

The World Goes to John

Crowds! Nothing is so confusing, so baffling, so apt to bring a sense of impenetrable mystery as vast gatherings of people. Sometimes they impress one as having the satanic threat of a Maricopa sidewinder—motionless, but ready to strike; then, again, so full of divine possibility that we can think of naught else save the singing multitude before the Great White Throne. Crowds are annoying to all human philosophy: "I hate the vulgar multitudes." They are used as false major and minor premises in a charlatan's syllogism, providing him a vicious eight-sheet conclusion of divine approval. They have often served as damnable yardsticks for groundlings to dismiss with contempt the day of small things. Crowds! There's no handle to take them by save the Grace of God. That Young Galilean alone was competent for the riddle—"When he saw the multitudes, he was moved with compassion on them."

No chapter in this Puritan monograph is so unwelcome, so needy of a guided treatment, so gratefully closed when completed—the story of the multitudes that gathered in London and elsewhere to hear the "Heir of the Puritans," from the time he accepted the New Park Street pastorate, as a boy of nineteen, until he died thirty-eight years later, at the age of fifty-seven. The very recording of these vast concourses has a dreadful, exalted monotony about it, causing one to meet with gratitude the few scanty records where attendance sagged.

There is blessed relief to find one month, for instance, when only seven joined the Tabernacle, and to hear a deacon say to Spurgeon, "This won't pay, Governor, running all this big place for seven new members in a month." It makes him seem like a brother to read that on December 19, 1858, though the weather was not bad, the Surrey Gardens' crowd "dwindled down to very small proportions and Mr. Spurgeon certainly appeared sad." Sounds refreshing, even if on the next Sunday, which was rainy, the crowd came back!

Let's herd this untamable set of crowd-records into a single chapter-corral, then ride on, having them safely penned up behind us. The Son of God was chary about statistics; just that–chary; frugal in emotional reactions. And he urged his followers to be like-minded: "In this rejoice not, that the spirits are subject unto you; but rather rejoice, because your names are written in heaven." The very memory of those monster gatherings year after year gives one a pathetic feeling of human frailty standing in the need of grace.

Almost at once when the nineteen-year-old boy began his ministry, the New Park Street Chapel was packed to the doors. What difference if it *were* hidden in South London–(who was it created that mouse-trap and beaten path bon mot?)–seats, aisles and window-sills were crowded, hundreds lingering at the door for crumbs from the banquet table. The hopelessly large chapel, seating twelve hundred, was now hopelessly small.

One night when the building was painfully

jammed, Spurgeon pointed to the wall behind the pulpit and said, "By faith the walls of Jericho fell down, and by faith this wall shall come down too!" A deacon protested; but the church did knock the wall down, at a cost of ten thousand dollars. During the period of repair, February 11 to May 27, 1855, they worshiped in Exeter Hall, in the Strand. It was a considerable auditorium, seating forty-five hundred. Elaborately stamped designs on walls and ceiling, complicated hanging gas-chandeliers, and a towering cliff of dummy gilt organ pipes back of the rostrum. But the crowds filled it as easily as New Park Street Chapel. For six Sunday evenings the streets were choked with people, vehicles retarded, and pedestrians compelled to go around side streets. This first experience was a dreadful trial for Spurgeon, as he had not yet developed the big-crowd voice. His voice often broke and sometimes practically failed. A glass of Chili vinegar on the pulpit proved a feeble ally for emergencies. In a year, however, he had mastered the secrets of speaking to the multitude, his throat becoming "macadamized." Susannah said, "As a master musician playing a priceless instrument, he could charm with notes of dulcet sweetness, or ring forth clarion notes of alarm."

The repair money was wasted. When they returned to the Chapel the overcrowding was worse than ever—halls, passages, side rooms chock-full—three thousand people packed into a fifteen-hundred-capacity building. They muddled through for a year, then in June, 1856, rehired Exeter Hall for

Sunday nights, holding morning services in the Chapel. And now—Exeter Hall was too small!

A bold plan was adopted to lease Surrey Music Hall, in the Royal Surrey Gardens. This was London's "largest, most commodious and most beautiful building, erected for public amusements, carnivals of wild beasts and wilder men." It accommodated ten to twelve thousand people. The news of this bold scheme ran through London like wild-fire.

On the afternoon of October 19, 1856, the crowd began gathering for the opening service; wild disorder, milling for seats; so that at evening service the hall was packed, and ten thousand more were outside. When Spurgeon saw it he was almost overwhelmed.

The service began, ran a few minutes, when suddenly a cry, "Fire! the galleries are giving away, the place is falling!" A terrible panic followed; seven were killed, many seriously injured. Spurgeon's grief over this almost unseated his reason. He was immediately hidden from the public; spent hours "in tears by day, and dreams of terror by night." A depression complex deepened upon him, from which he never fully recovered.

But the disaster itself increased the crowds. Charles Haddon Spurgeon became a world figure over night. On Sunday he was a local celebrity of South London, a "South of the Slot" hero; the next week he was a world figure. All London now wanted to hear him.

Then a tide of slander and vilification set in; newspaper cartoons, bitter editorials, and, more difficult to bear, bitter criticism of other ministers. Alas! nothing is more venomous than corroding pettiness of jealous clergymen! High visibility has its penalties—"A city set on a hill cannot be hid." Thus was Joseph shot at by the archers. But his bow abode in strength, *and the crowds increased!*

In two weeks he had himself sufficiently in hand to preach again. This time, however, for prudence sake, they used Surrey Hall mornings instead of evenings. Crowds greater than ever! For a period of over three years, November, 1856, to December, 1859, an average of ten thousand *every Sunday!* Lines of horses and carriages choked the streets. Cabbies in London shouted to prospective fares, "Over the river to Charlie?"

Outdoor preaching now attracted him. Also, the cities of England, Scotland, Ireland, and Wales arranged services in their largest buildings. The passing years are monotonous in monster statistics. An average of eight to twelve outside services a week, all over the Empire, and Holland and France. Depressing records of multitudes that would fill a quarto.

The Metropolitan Tabernacle was completed in March, 1861. The succeeding thirty-one years saw an average of five thousand people assembled there every Sunday, morning and evening. Once a quarter, Spurgeon asked his regular attendants to stay away from the next service. They did so; but the vast Tabernacle was jammed just the same, with an altogether different crowd, "the unreached masses."

By 1867 the Tabernacle had become tawdry under the mauling of millions of hands and feet. During the refurbishing, Agricultural Hall, Islington, was used five Sunday mornings, March to April, 1867. It was a giant building, big as a Zeppelin hangar, the same kind of a circular roof, with vast areas of glass to the sky, each sectored end being a colossal window appearing as expansive as Half Dome in Yosemite Valley. Greater records! Twenty thousand average attendance!

The all-time attendance record, "the greatest crowd ever addressed by a gospel preacher," was set October 7, 1857, in Spurgeon's twenty-third year. The occasion was a fast-day service held in the central transcept of the Cyclopean Crystal Palace, a building so large that it was "apparently unenclosed for vastness." By turnstile count, 23,654 persons were present. An interesting side-light showing the strain of this service is found in the record that after it was over Spurgeon slept from Wednesday night to Friday morning!

Another interesting incident in connection with this Agricultural Hall meeting was Spurgeon's private afternoon acoustical test in the empty building. He lifted his golden voice and cried, "Behold the Lamb of God which taketh away the sin of the world." A workman in a high gallery heard the voice, was smitten with conviction, put down his tools, went home, and after a season of spiritual struggle, found peace and life by beholding the Lamb of God. How truly did the young prophet "magnify" his God!

Crowds! Cosmopolitan, too! The élite were there; such cut as Gladstone, Ruskin, Shaftesbury; nobility; Queen Victoria in disguise; famous globetrotters; statesmen, soldiers, authors, artists, ministers and captains of industry; rich man, poor man, beggar man, thief; factory girls, artisans, street women, ne'er-do-wells and drunks; farmers, carters' boys, shopkeepers and dairy maids.

Preeminently these crowds were common people. In this Spurgeon had greater delight. He wrote his brother: "The Lord Mayor, a Jew has been . . . the Chief Commissioner of Police also . . . but better still, some thieves, thimbleriggers (shell game), harlots; . . and some are now in the church . . . as also a right honorable hot-potatoe man, who is prominently known as a 'hot Spurgeonite.'" The costermongers–push-cart gentry–whose livelihood depended on good lungs, said of him, "I never! Stunnin'! Wot a woice! Would make a good coster!"

The church grew mightily. By January, 1855, it had risen to 313. There was a net increase of 282 in 1855, 265 in 1856, bringing the total to 860–425 per cent, increase in less than three years. The first ten years 3,569 were baptized. In 1875 the membership was 4,417. When Spurgeon began in London, Baptists were the conies among Israel; at his death, in 1892, the membership was 5,307. During his entire pastorate a total of 14,700 were added: 10,800 by baptism, 2,933 by letter, 947 by profession and 20 by restoration.[1] A general awakening was noted in all denominations. When

---

[1] Figures supplied the author by Elder Rounds, November 20, 1933.

he died, Baptists had become a world force. Draw your own conclusions.

Crowds! They mean terrible responsibilities. Heavy burdens settled on his young shoulders. That crushing strain of always looking into an ocean of faces, while his heart hungered for sylvan glades and the sky-sung ecstacy of nightingales. "Persons," he said, "I fear not at all; a multitude makes me tremble." "But," adds Fullerton, "it's the race-horse not the cart-horse that trembles on the verge of the task."

It is no light matter to be John crying in the wilderness with the world coming out to hear you. It involves tensions that may be met only in the consecration garments of humility—camels' hair; leathern girdle; a rugged spiritual aliment reminding one of Calvary, locusts and wild honey; and an unvarying message of self-effacement—"I am not He; not worthy to unlatch His shoes. Behold the Lamb of God! *He* taketh away the sin of the world."

Crowds! The whole enigma has but one adequate approach, the one Spurgeon gave it. The last service held in Surrey Gardens was December 11, 1859.[2] His text was Acts 20:26, "I am pure from the blood of all men." His sentences were Dantesque in power: "In God's name, I beseech you, flee to Christ for refuge! Shall there be any of you, whom I shall see on my death-bed, who shall

[2] The church returned to Exeter Hall for the remaining six Sundays before the Tabernacle was finished, leaving Surrey Gardens because its management was about to lease it out as a honky-tonk. It failed miserably after the church left, their rentals having kept it going.

charge me with being unfaithful? Shall these eyes be haunted with visions of men whom I have amused, but into whose heart I have never sought to convey the truth? Shall I lie there, and shall these mighty congregations pass in dreary panorama before me, and as they subside, shall each one curse me as being unfaithful? God avert that worst of ills—unfaithfulness—from my head! I pray you, in Christ's stead, be ye reconciled to God!"

Age 18

Age 33

Age 65

Three Studies of Susannah

XII

Bowstring

As unto the cord the bow is,
So unto the man is woman.
Though she bends him, she obeys him,
Though she draw him, yet she follows.
Useless each without the other.

*—H. W. Longfellow, New England Puritan and
descendant of the Puritan Longfellow (1650-1698), of
Hampshire, England.*

She delights in her husband, in his person, his character, his affection; to her, he is not only the chief and foremost of mankind, but in her eyes, he is all in all. Her heart's love belongs to him and to him only. He is her little world, her Paradise, her choice treasure. She is glad to sink her individuality in his. She seeks no renown for herself; his honor is reflected upon her, and she rejoices in it. She will defend his name with her dying breath; safe enough is he where she can speak for him. His smiling gratitude is all the reward she seeks. Even in her dress she thinks of him, and considers nothing beautiful which is distasteful to him. He has many objects in life, some of which she does not quite understand; but she believes in them all, and anything she can do to promote them, she delights to perform. . . Such a wife, as a true spouse, realizes the model marriage relation, and sets forth what our oneness with the Lord ought to be!—C. H. S.' *veiled description of Susannah.*

BOWSTRING

However heavily our chariot wheels may have dragged in previous chapters, here, at least, they shall run and be glorified. Enter the heroine, Susannah Thompson—a spirit cast in a yet fairer mold than Prince Charming himself. We have respectfully penetrated the shadows of Christlike self-effacement in which she selected to hide herself; we have refused to be blinded by the calcium brilliance history sheds upon the figure of her husband; and, as a bounty upon patience, have found Susannah to be one of the most exalted of the daughters of Eve. Our personal astonishment in England's permitting the Puritan Library to be carried off to a Missouri Main Street is exceeded only by the fact that this exotic British Deborah has had no scribe to give the world her full-length portrait. Her life is a veritable Eldorado, with not a literary claim-stake in sight. We set ours down, right here, and promise, "if the sands of the glass fail not," humbly to present her radiant story in *Susannah of Westwood.*

In every area, she was "one of the notable women to whom the nations come." Her mental and spiritual life were marked by such poetic temper that her very sentences have the inimitable fragrance of jessamine. Had she not deliberately chosen to sink herself in Tirshatha, she could have mounted the levels of Elizabeth Barrett Browning.

Tirshatha, by the way, is the name of endearment with which she addressed the Heir of the Puritans. It was an ancient Persian term signifying "Your Reverence." Spurgeon, to her, was always Tirshatha, from the gay wedding bells in New Park Street Church to the lonely bereavement of Mentone.

The love-life of the Spurgeons is a treasury of lavender and old lace, a thing of such rare beauty that one does not find its equal until he reaches the level of the Brownings of Wimpole Street. How much of the concept, "Charles Haddon Spurgeon," was really Susannah, none but the angels can determine. We shall not try. We dismiss that part of the problem by saying—Three forces made the Heir of the Puritans: the Young Son of God, the Shadow of the Broad Brim, and—Susannah of Westwood.

When the young Waterbeach pastor of nineteen preached that first Sunday in London, December 18, 1853, one of the small number present at the evening service was a charming young lady of eighteen—Susannah! She was of slight stature, her oval face framed in long chestnut curls. Had she weighed a pound more, she might have been a bit heavy; had she weighed a pound less, some might have thought her too slender. Sensitive tapering fingers; the adorable little grace of marked luster coming into her hazel eyes when interest was challenged. That night she wore a snug-fitting black bodice, slightly open at the throat, giving way for a little pendant, and bordered by a small, frilly white collar of lace. Ah, she was a man's woman, every bit of her dainty five foot three!

It should be said here that Susannah all her life had that captivating combination of physical charm coupled with a deeply spiritual nature. Doctor Campbell covered the opening services at the new Metropolitan Tabernacle in 1861 for a Baptist paper. He thus described detail of the first baptismal service, April 9. (Susannah was then twenty-six, and the mother of two little boys):

> "The interest in that first baptismal service was overpowering. There was the young orator, the idol of the assembly, in the water, with a countenance of light. And there on the pathway was Susannah, a most prepossessing young lady, with courtly dignity and inimitable modesty, kindly leading forward the trembling sisters in succession to her husband!"

But on that first December night she was not at all impressed with the boy preacher. We have a record of her mental reactions:

"So this is his so-called eloquence! It does not impress me. What a painful countrified manner! Will he ever quit making flourishes with that terrible blue silk handkerchief! And his hair—why, he looks like a barber's assistant!"

He amused her; it was trying to keep a straight face; and he shocked her, too. Just think of a preacher asserting Christians are "living stones, joined with the vermillion cement of Christ's blood."

Whether they met or not that evening, neither could afterward remember. But during May, 1854, she did meet him several times in the home of the Olneys. She was not yet a church-member, though her interests had been previously aroused during special meetings. She began regularly to hear Spurgeon preach. And then on a day—well, her heart hungered to find the Christ of God. We are content to let prosaic psychologists take her emotion apart in order to determine how much of this awakening was centered in the young dominie, and how much in the Young Redeemer. Some of us know well enough that the partition in holy love is exceedingly hard to place. Heaven-born affection has evermore had a queer way of leading lovers to the Greatest of All Lovers.

Susannah's deep concern of heart was reported to the young pastor. He therefore sent a present to the awakened young lady—his first gift. Shades of the Broad Brim! it was a copy of *Pilgrim's Progress!* On the fly-leaf was inscribed in his best holograph, "Miss Thompson, with desires for her progress in the blessed pilgrimage, from C. H. Spurgeon, April 20, 1854." A little later she gave, as one of her first gifts to him, a complete set of John Calvin! Susannah said, with charming naïvety: "I don't think my beloved had at that time any other thought concerning me than to help a struggling soul heavenward." Maybe she was right; but some of us who well know the heart of a man when it finds its woman are no little dubious.

On June 10 they attended the brilliant opening of the Crystal Palace, decorated with Miami palms in great tubs. They sat together in the grand-stand. Spurgeon as usual carried a book. This time, however, it was not deep divinity; it contained poems on love and marriage. He had her read one which he pointed out. And as she read, he asked in a soft, low voice, "Do you pray for him who is to be your husband?"

Love has strange ways; this ought to be proof. Susannah said she never could remember if she answered. But there was a fast-beating heart, a tell-tale blush and downcast eyes. From that moment, a very quiet and subdued little maiden sat at the young pastor's side. A brilliant procession was passing around the Palace, but she had no eyes for it.

The communications between the two from that time are models of beauty. The young pastor was under double tension; he was a responsible soul-surgeon, and he was a man who had fallen in love. On February 1, 1855, he baptized her in the New Park Street Chapel baptistry.

They began to meet oftener. On August 2, 1854–Susannah speaking–"loving looks, and tender tones and clasping hands gave way to verbal confession!" At just about this time the walls came down, that is, New Park Street Chapel was enlarged. Susannah collected five hundred dollars for the building fund!

Well, we'll just have to let them marry. Particularly so when we see that the best was yet to be;

their romance never soared so loftily *before* as it did *after* their home was set up.

God had made them for each other; no further use in delaying the wedding! On January 8, 1856, there was a memorable early morning ceremony at New Park Street Chapel, performed by the Rev. Alexander Fletcher. The auditorium was full of people and scores were in the streets. A Paris honeymoon of ten days followed. And when the packet boat bore them back to England she whispered to him:

"O Tirshatha! Often before have I been in Paris. But, this time it has been ten times as charming in my eyes, *because you were with me!*"

The young couple immediately took up residence at 217 New Kent Road. It should be said that Susannah had no small measure of heartache to master, for she found it was serious business to be married to a public man whose presence was being sought everywhere, and whose time even in London was never his own. Spurgeon's heavy duties and consequent abstraction nearly caused a rift in courtship days. She said: "When he came over to visit me on Mondays, he corrected the proof sheets of his weekly sermon, and I had to learn to be quiet." Once at a public service he altogether forgot her, and an indignant young miss flew home in tears to her mother. The mother was wise in the ways of men; Susannah must forgive Charles. Susannah did. Gradually she mastered her self-interests; and she realized that however busy Tirshatha might be, his heart was always dreaming of her. On September 20, 1856, the twin sons, Charles and James, were born.

In 1857, the Spurgeons moved to "Helensburgh," in Nightingale Lane, a lovely old remodeled ten-room house in rural surroundings. At the rear was a fine, typical English garden. Immediately, Susannah designated the best room for her husband's growing library. Her health began to fail in 1866, and in 1868 she broke down completely. For sixteen years she remained an invalid, unable even to attend church again until "Tirshatha's" fiftieth birthday, diamond jubilee, June 18, 1884.

In 1869 the old Helensburgh house was completely pulled down and a lovely two-story house of gray pressed brick erected in its place. The principal part of the cost was defrayed by a few of Spurgeon's most liberal and devoted helpers in the Tabernacle. The Spurgeons lived in Brighton while William Higgs was building the new Helensburgh. They occupied the new home for eleven years, until "every nook became sacred to us."

By 1880 Nightingale Lane lost its rural aspect, the smoke pall becoming so dense that a removal seemed advisable for the sake of Susannah. Accidentally, Spurgeon discovered the old estate, Westwood, on the Southern Heights. Providentially, he was able to sell Helensburgh at just the right time, and practically purchased Westwood with the price of sale.

Westwood was Spurgeon's home until his death in 1892; and here Susannah remained until her death, October 22, 1903. Westwood became known all over the civilized earth. Famous men journeyed thither to visit with the Heir of the Puritans. It had nine and one-half acres of woodland and lawns, a garden, a little lake, and a bowling green. Why shouldn't Tirshatha enjoy bowls? It was a Puritan pastime!

The palatial house, on a little rise of ground, tree-framed, had a fine corner tower; within, there was a glassed fernery, rosery and vinery; a master bedroom up-stairs, as well as guest-rooms. Two large rooms down-stairs, with French doors in the outside walls, overlooked the garden. Susannah immediately said, "These shall be Tirshatha's study."

During the early years of their married life Susannah was very active in all the work at Tabernacle; it was much a question with the thousands of the congregation as to which was more beloved, the young orator or his gracious young wife. Several times they toured Europe together. Her fair hands laid the first stone of the Pastors' College House, at the request of those who raised the funds; whereupon "twenty-six little girls in white, advanced one by one, with purses . . . a token of their parents' affectionate rejoicing at her presence!"[1] The first twelve years of their home life were without a cloud, save that "Tirshatha's health was not the best, and she must see to him carefully."

Then came the fatal year 1868, when at the age of thirty-three she became practically a helpless invalid. It must be recorded, as an evidence of the grace of God, that the beauty of the Spurgeon home rose to new heights upon their misfortune. Spurgeon once said that "we never knew fully the sym-

---

[1] Schindler.

The Gates

Front Facade

Study

Views of Westwood

pathy of Christ, till there was a loved one over whom we must agonize day after day." A deepened tenderness came into his public ministry. Many hours he spent at her bedside, reviewing every little memory of foreign travel. His own health soon failed so rapidly that, during many subsequent years, he was each autumn forced to flee London fogs to Mentone. It was to each of them a heart-breaking annual separation. Charles' real love letters to Susannah began, dated from Mentone, fifteen years after their marriage.

She said, "His letters were always those of a devoted lover, the brook never dried up, the stream grew deeper and broader." Every Mentone post bore missives to Helensburgh or Westwood: "Twenty years have passed. My heart flies to you. I love you now as then, only multiplied many times. I have served the Lord far more and never less for your sweet companionship! . . Bless your dear heart! . . You are the precise form in which God would make a woman for such a man as I . . . I leave off ere the paper is covered."

Gladstone once explained his great capacity for work by saying, "I am happy in my home." Never was a woman of greater inspiration to a man than was Susannah. She read to him Saturday nights, even in days of invalidism, from his blessed Puritans. At the beginning of their married life, she sacrificed common comforts so that Tirshatha might start his college. Many times he came home from the great Tabernacle meetings exhausted and in the grip of depression. Then she would read to him from Baxter's *Reformed Pastor*–"he would weep at my feet, and I would weep too; not because he had really done poorly, but because I felt sorry for him."

In every mauling depression Spurgeon hurried to Susannah for comfort. After the Surrey Hall tragedy, she alone kept his "sanity upon the throne." At this far day, it brings a heart-throb to read her words upon the beginning of his mental recovery: "We walked together . . . he anguished . . . I amazed. . . Then he stopped suddenly and turned to me *with the old sweet light in his eyes.*" What she meant to him may be gleaned from a letter he wrote her in 1889, during "The Down Grade": "You are as an angel of God to me. . . Bravest of women, strong in the faith, you have ministered unto me . . . God bless thee out of the Seventh Heaven!"

It was during her invalid days that she started the famous Book Fund, through which thousands of poor ministers of all faiths welcomed volumes given to them. It came about in this way:

Susannah had acquired one of those typically feminine peculiarities, unfathomable to the mere male, but altogether adorable–she saved every five-shilling piece she got. Why? Why *five*-shilling pieces? We give it up. Lo, we have too many such unsolved variants near at hand to undertake more. *But she saved them.*

When Spurgeon published the first volume of *Lectures to My Students*, she said, "Oh, Tirshatha, I wish a copy could be placed with every minister in England." He answered, "Then why not do it? How much will you give?" She promptly brought forth a little army of five-shilling pieces. It provided sufficient to buy one hundred copies. Thus began her Book Fund. It was by means of this enterprise that her heart found victory and peace, despite her anguish. She thus explains her change of front:

At the end of a dreary London day, she lay suffering on her couch, some of the darkness in her soul. Why did her Lord thus deal with his child? "For a while," she writes, "silence reigned in the little room broken only by the crackling of an oak log on the fireplace. Suddenly I heard a sweet, soft sound, a little clear musical note, like the tender trill of a robin. 'What can that be?' I said to my companion. We listened, and again the soft plaintive note. Tirshatha exclaimed, 'It comes from the log on the fire.' The fire was letting loose the imprisoned music, garnered up by the old oak when soft sunlight flecked his tender leaves with gold. We are like this old log. We should give forth no melodious sounds were it not for the fire!"

Thus the fire in her own life brought melody into the homes of hundreds of poor ministers; and, from them, the melody came back to her. A special room was fitted up in Westwood as the shipping department. The little Lady of the Manse in the next twenty years mailed gratuitously more than two hundred thousand volumes, many of which were Tirshatha's, especially his *Treasury of David.* She wrote two books, *Ten Years of My Life* and *Ten Years After,* both accounts of the Book Fund. They are exceedingly worth while; try to get one. I've been unable to, although I have had the best book hunters in America on the trail. She also wrote *Westwood Papers*, reports that still are almost like fiction in beauty and interest.

In the early days of February, 1892, Susannah returned from Mentone with the casket of her beloved husband. Westwood seemed strangely large and empty. Memories everywhere! Then in her grief, she remembered a time of lesser heart-break, long ago when her world was young.

In one of those "dear dead days beyond recall," as her boyish husband was leaving Helensburgh, tears would trickle down her cheeks in spite of her efforts; everything seemed so empty when he was away.

"Seeing me look so sad, he tenderly said, 'What! crying over your lamb, wifie? Do you think the children of Israel stood and wept over the lamb they laid on His altar?'"

Then the heart of Susannah found peace in tears. She looked at the great portrait of Tirshatha over the mantel and sobbed: "Ah, sweetheart! was there ever one like thee? In all these forty years I knew thee, thou wert most tender, gracious! And now I am parted from thee, not for a few days only, as in that long ago time, but 'until the day break and the shadows flee away!' I think I hear thy loving voice saying again, 'Don't cry over your lamb, wifie,' as I try to give thee up, ungrudgingly to God—not without tears—ah, no, that is not possible; but with that full surrender of heart which makes the sacrifice acceptable in His sight."

XIII

HEIR OF THE PURITANS

The Puritans were men whose minds derived a peculiar character from the daily contemplation of superior beings and eternal interests. Not content with acknowledging, in general terms, an overruling Providence, they habitually ascribed every event to the will of a Great Being, for whose power nothing was too vast, for whose inspection nothing was too minute. To know Him, to serve Him, to enjoy Him, was with them the great end of existence. . . They recognized no title to superiority but His favor; and, confident of that favor, they despised all the accomplishments and all the dignities of the world. If they were unacquainted with the works of philosophers and poets, they were deeply read in the oracles of God. . . Legions of ministering angels had charge over them. Their palaces were houses not made with hands. . . On the rich and the eloquent, on nobles and priests, they looked down with contempt. . . It was for Him that the sun had been darkened, that the rocks had been rent, that the dead had risen, that all nature had shuddered at the sufferings of her expiring God. . . The intensity of their feelings on one subject made them tranquil on every other . . . cleared their minds from every vulgar passion.–*Macaulay's "Milton."*

Heir of the Puritans

The servants of God since time's beginning stand in one or another of two types, whose differences are those of genus rather than species. The people of one group, lovable for the most part, capable, industrious, are nevertheless lacking in that certain elusive quality that gives radiant unity to an individual. The modern psychologist diagnoses their cases as: "imperfect synthesis." The people of the other group, much fewer in number, possess, each of them, a something over and above; a something not to be isolated in an inventory of abilities. Yet its possession underwrites the doing of impossibles: changing the leopard's spots; transmutation of baser metals into gold; putting hands on God's throne and broken humanity and drawing them together.

We shall not get lost in a rationale upon these Prometheans for an Arctic interval, excepting to say that their sword was bathed in heaven. The Old Testament remarks simply, "The Spirit of Jehovah came upon them." The New Testament says, "Baptized with the Holy Ghost and with fire"; while certain of yesterday's moderns tagged it "Divine Afflatus," an unhappy label, smelling of Latin smoke.

It is a matter of gratitude that the pivots upon which it seemeth good to swing this chapter are very simple in fashion; honest wrought-iron axes, whose specifications may be set in a phrase: Each of those men who through faith subdued kingdoms, reached his spiritual integration in the same way; a prolonged brooding upon the Word of God *and* the writings of some Christian Great-heart who himself had fire. Luther's zeal that set the world ablaze came to him from a three-year vigil with the Scriptures *and* the writings of Augustine. Calvin lighted his torch in the same way. So did Whitefield. The Puritans, whose description by Macaulay merits a hundred readings, obtained their peculiar character by long, unhurried exposure to the Bible *and* the writings of John Calvin. Always, these men of signal radiance came to their heritage through the Bible, *and* someone who knew it well. And Charles Haddon Spurgeon received his baptism of fire from hours without end of communing with the Bible at his right hand *and* the books of Puritan divinity at his left.

This illustrates a curious fact in spiritual psychology, which moderns call "triangulation." The principal rests in the will of God, and finds reflection in the Scripture, "Not forsaking the assembling of ourselves together." (Strange perversion to restrict *this* to *church-attendance!*) Apostolic fire runs only in alternating current about a holy triangle: God, ourselves, and someone else. Leave that "someone else" out, and the lines are down. What a curious thing, this divine gift! One may go to a retreat and come away with "a transient urge": he will lose it again next week. To keep it, one must meditate time without stint upon the Scriptures *and* the fiery oracles of those who knew them best.

Now, the fire-line from Pentecost seems to be one simple channel. "You may take a step from Paul to Augustine, and then from Augustine to Calvin, and then—you may keep your foot up a good while before you find such another. Augustine was the great mine out of which Calvin digged his mental wealth" (C. H. S.). The Puritans got their patterns from the same sources, the Bible *and* Calvin.

Spurgeon was completely fashioned by the Puritans, so much so that the phrase-makers of the nineteenth century tried to mirror him in Puritan clauses. A London paper said he was "A Puritan born out of time" (very poor). Another said he was "A Puritan bound in buckram" (a little better). Many tried to title him, "The Last of the Puritans." He was not, and never will be; others of that stamp are yet to come. Better still is this new phrase, "Charles Haddon Spurgeon, the *Heir* of the Puritans." No singularity can be charged against this epithet, inasmuch as whosoever will may be joint heirs with him.

The seventeenth-century Puritans produced a family of spiritual giants, scores of great intellects who went unobserved in the midst of the mammoth settings of their day: Ness, Hawker, Dickinson, Mayor, Crosby, Day, Charnock, Manton, Brooks, Flavel, Jermin, Harmer, Gurnall, Sedgwick, Bussy, Knolly, Binning, Banbury, Calderott, Longfellow, Poole, Haak. These men were prolific publishers; all of them experts in the deeper things of the Word. They possessed a discernment in the finer points of Christianity such as is matched only by John Ruskin's insight of nature's delicate moods. Kiddie-car intellects of succeeding years have been appalled by these mountain men, dismissing them with the ragged defense-technique of spiritual inertia: "They are narrow, hair-splitting, heavy, involved!" Spurgeon fell in love with the volumes of Puritan divinity by the time he was six years old and reveled in their racy writings for half a century. His was a virtuoso's passion running the whole scale from the ponderous duodecimos of his grandfather's manse to the royal octavos in the Old Curiosity Shop. Early in life he started a collection. He ransacked bookstalls and kept an eagle eye on booksellers' catalogs for any he did not possess.

His discernment in these books became as delicate as a china-collector's: "It is easy to tell a Puritan book by even its shape, and the type." He hunted originals, not cut reprints: "I harbor a prejudice against all new editions, and a preference for the originals, even though they wander about in sheepskins and goatskins, and are shut up in the heaviest of board."

So great was his love for his Puritans that he had Susannah read them to him while they were engaged! Susannah said: "I heard his dear voice explain what I couldn't understand, condensing into short sentences whole pages of these discursive old divines, and pressing from them all the richest nectar of their hidden sweetness." The two of them in courtship days actually issued a book of Puritan anthology, *Smooth Stones Taken from Ancient Brooks*. (Brooks was a Puritan.) So assiduously did he collect that at his death in 1892 nearly seven thousand Puritan volumes were in his library.

Part of the Puritan Library in a Library Corner at Westwood
(Now owned by William Jewell College, Liberty, Missouri)

We stop to note some interesting facts about this collection. It was offered for sale in 1905 for $2,500! England was napping. Dr. J. T. M. Johnson, John E. Franklin, President John Priest Greene, and Dr. J. E. Cook, of Missouri, swiftly raised three thousand dollars (price was ante-ed) and bought the entire lot—fifty cents a volume! Dr. J. W. Thirtle of London supervised the packing, in thirty-eight cases lined with water-proof canvas. He shipped them on the *S. S. Cuba* Saturday, December 16, 1905, billed to New Orleans, thence by the Illinois Central to Kansas City, and fifteen miles farther to a little country town called Liberty, where they arrived in January, 1906.

There they are today, in William Jewell College, undivided—and almost unknown! A priceless collection of rare volumes, stately folios, duodecimos, quartos; all marked with Spurgeon's own hand; a set never to be duplicated and never rivaled. Strange! if any one now wishes to drink from the wells of Puritan divinity, he will need to go to this quiet little Missouri village. Who would ever have thought of finding Spurgeon's well-thumbed books "west of the Mississippi River"? In that collection there is a priceless copy of his *Commenting and Commentators*, annotated in his own hand for the improvement of later editions. There is also the *Comprehensive Bible* which he used in New Park Street—by any standard of rare book appraisals its present value should be five thousand dollars.

How completely Spurgeon was shaped by the Puritans is the theme of this entire book. His mind became steeped in their seventeenth-century language.

They taught him to say exactly what he wanted to say in pure Anglo-Saxon, so that he did speak "Market English" all his days. He knew more about Puritanism than the Puritans themselves. In Mentone retirement he always carried a Puritan volume on his walks. Their outlook became his outlook in all points–the finality of God's Word, the right of private judgment, separation of church and state, liberty of conscience, and the supremacy of the spiritual in human life.

From all this he had no desire to change. To him the greatest compliment he ever received was intended as a withering criticism: "Here is a man who has not moved an inch forward in all his ministry, and at the close of the nineteenth century is teaching the theology of the first century."

His ministerial heroes were likewise men who had lighted their torches from Puritan fires. George Müller, on their first meeting, in Bristol, November, 1854, so moved him that "I could not speak a word for the life of me." This was the real beginning of the Tabernacle. Immediately on arriving home he said to his people: "We will try the power of faith here. We may have a tabernacle of faith as well as an orphanage of faith." John Knox swayed him as a tempest. "Oh, God," he cried, "we want John Knox back again; not mild, gentle men! Fiery Knox, even though he should ding our pulpits into blads!" Once he declared, "If there were wanted two more apostles, I do not believe there could be found two more fit than George Whitefield and John Wesley!"

George Whitefield! Here we find another Puritan derivative who came to be Spurgeon's greatest human example. In his copy of Whitefield's sermons there is this inscription: "C. H. Spurgeon, who admires Whitefield as the chief of preachers." Once he said of him, "He lived! Whitefield was all life, fire, wing, force. My own model, if I may have such a thing, in due subordination to my Lord, is George Whitefield."

The influence of these knights of fire, wing and force has strange power over all who meet them. Such was Spurgeon himself. He became to thousands a part of that mystic combination, the Word of God *and* the words of someone who is wise therein. Great men were content to light their candles at his. Once a year Bishop Thorold spent a day in prayer and communion with Spurgeon, to get into a right state of heart. James Denny had the conventional paucity of mere brilliance until he started to read Spurgeon's sermons—then, he wrote that classic—*The Death of Christ.*

Shaftesbury, Gladstone, Livingstone, Wilberforce, Nightingale, Cuyler, A. T. Pierson, Gough and even John Ruskin rejoiced in the glow of Spurgeon's presence. Mark Guy Pearse said, "He winds me up like an eight-day clock." And Dwight L. Moody frankly confessed that his fires came from the Bible *and* Spurgeon—"Everything he ever said, I read. My eyes just feast on him. John Wesley lives more today than ever; so does Whitefield; so does John Knox. If God can use Mr. Spurgeon, why should he not use the rest of us."

The more we proceed in this investigation, the more do we realize that Spurgeon was indeed the Heir of the Puritans. He gave the clue to his whole mental and spiritual process when he wrote of Manton: "Thus my communing with that great Puritan ends in my clearing his house of all his pictures, and hanging them up in new frames in my own." Hear also these bold words in an address at the Pastors' College:

"We endeavor to teach the Scriptures, but, as everybody else claims to do the same, we say distinctly that our theology is Puritanic. We stand by the old ways. We prefer Manton to Maurice, Charnock to Robertson, and Owen to Voysey. Believing that the Puritanic school embodied more of gospel truth than any other since the apostles, we continue in the same line of things; and by God's help, hope to have a share in that revival of Evangelical doctrine which is as sure to come as the Lord himself!"

Spurgeon was right. We are not through with the Puritans yet. Great awakenings are always delayed, awaiting the coming of men whose souls are inflamed by long exposure to God's Word and the words of men who best understand it. Richard S. Storrs wrote: "The Puritan conception of life has always been that of a battle and a march under watchful heavens, toward superlative issues, with great destinies involved." To which Fullerton added: "There are abiding elements in Puritan thought and practice which are bound to reappear *whenever* the problems of life and the relations of God to man are seriously considered."

XIV

A Puritan Arrowsmith

Now we know that sticks are not by nature arrows; they do not grow so, but they are made so; by nature they are knotty and rugged, but by art they are smooth and handsome.–*George Swinnock (1627-1673)*.

Beware of running about from this meeting to that, contributing your share to the general blowing up of windbags. Your pulpit preparations are your first business. The honest minister puts an arrow on the string, and the Holy Spirit sends it right home. Reach down one of the Puritans, and thoroughly study the work, and you will find yourself mentally active and full of motion.–C. H. S.

Elijah's servant went once, and saw nothing; therefore he was commanded to look seven times. So may you look lightly upon the Scripture and see nothing; meditate often upon it, and there you shall see a light like the light of the sun. *–Joseph Caryl (1647)*.

Pray over the Scripture, it is as the treading of grapes in the wine vat, the threshing of corn on the barn floor, the melting of gold from the ore.–C. H. S.

A Puritan Arrowsmith

The mind of the Puritan was thoroughly "Bibline." His words for the common facts of life, therefore, had the freshness and vigor of meadows of Bethlehem. He read Micah 4:6-8 and Jeremiah 6:27 and called his pulpit "The Tower of the Flock." He remembered 2 Chronicles 26:14-16, envisioning *himself* to be one of the skilful men on the towers, and thereafter referred to his sermons as his arrows. He read Psalm 7:13 and decided his main business to be that of an arrowsmith who fashioned fiery shafts. Some may feel contemptuous of such make-believe, and call it infantile; but we remember reading somewhere that the dainty dreams of child-soul have close affinity to the Kingdom of Heaven.

Whatever else may have had high importance in Spurgeon's life, preaching was Mount Whitney in the Sierra Range of his labors. He so regarded it. Susannah said: "His whole heart was absorbed in it, all his spiritual force was engaged in it, all the intellectual power with which God so richly endowed him was pressed into this glorious service." It is my own conviction that his is the greatest figure that lifts itself on the homiletic skyline since Paul the tent-maker. How many different sermons he published may never be known; early research indicated the number to be 2,241; later information shows the right figure to be over 3,500, published in seventy-five distinct volumes. To read one a day would occupy over ten years of time!

Boys who, finding power-house doors open, enter to marvel over the great machines, have no more thrilling experience than one who peers into Spurgeon's armoury, and watches his skilled blows beat out the arrows of God by the quiverful, and then beholds him shoot, as he opens the window eastward (2 Kings 13:17). Let us observe his procedure in arrow-making; and may it be of as much profit to him who reads as it hath been to him who writes.

Begin with "stick-gathering, barb-finding and feather-questing," as Sibbe would put it; and you will behold Spurgeon among his books. His range of reading was like all other aspects of his life—unbelievably vast. "He was acquainted with all literature, biography, science, theology, history, art, poetry." He read all of Shakespeare's plays, some of them many times. He read rapidly. He made it a point to read half a dozen of the hardest books weekly. Behind this valorous reading was a youthful resolve: "I am bound to give myself unto reading, and study and prayer, and not to grieve the Spirit by unthought-of effusion." "He would sit down to five or six large books, and master them at one sitting and his memory didn't fail him on what he read." The day he perused Drummond's *Natural Law in the Spiritual World,* he went through four or five other books—and passed a friendly test thereon imposed by the incredulous W. T. Stead. It was an experience to hear him read aloud from Ruskin or Carlyle. World geography he had at his finger-tips.

He often sent his secretary to the British Museum to look up a subject, such as olive-trees. Bulky results would be distilled into a few simple sentences.

His chief book was, however, the Bible: "I should like always to be reading my Bible." Armitage felt that the hidings of his power lay in the hours beyond number in Mentone when he read the Bible from the sheer love thereof. Perhaps Spurgeon himself intended this when he said, "It is blessed to eat into the very soul of the Bible until, at last, you come to talk in scriptural language, and your spirit is flavored with the words of the Lord, so that your blood is *Bibline* and the very essence of the Bible flows from you. Hundreds of times have I surely felt that presence of God in the page of Scripture." No wonder James Stalker wrote of him, "To find his match in command of simple and powerful Anglo-Saxon, you have in England to go back to John Bunyan." I have checked scores of Scripture references not even marked as such in one of his sermons. I tell you this man preached the gospel. It was not against such as he that Carlyle aimed his blistering criticism: "The most enthusiastic evangelists do not preach a gospel, but keep describing how it should and might be preached."

Yet his reading was generally innocent of any special objective, homiletical or otherwise. His aim was simply to "fill the cask and keep it full." To him, reading with so naïve a motive as to feather his arrows, was to put a strain on information, giving his utterance the quality of an examination paper. If sermons were but drawn from a full cask, they would have the priceless quality of spontaneity. His temper could not endure the hand-to-mouth type of sermonizing. He did not even read the Bible that way.

How well did this method work out, in his case at least? When he was young, men noted his giant stride and wondered, "Will he last?" To which Edwin Paxton Hood replied, "Why not? There is apparently no strain in the production of these discourses; they bear every appearance of being spontaneous talkings . . . from a full and overflowing spring within him."

Susannah said (and thanks be for this little lady of the manse, because of all writers about him she alone has spiritually interpreted her husband): "While the dear Pastor was traveling, either at home or abroad, he always had his note-book . . . jotted down everything likely to be of service . . . incidents that could be used as illustrations being specially preserved."

Before beginning a study of his dramatic technique in sermon-building, let us note a few generalities as to his preaching. He employed every means to develop his style and ability. He always spoke extempore Monday night before his great prayer-service, "to keep him ready," selecting some topic that had been uppermost in his thoughts during the day. As for notes, he never permitted himself much more than half a page, because if he made them longer, he desired to make them longer still, until the extemporaneous quality of preaching bid fair to disappear. He must remain able to think on his feet. He spoke at the average rate of one hundred and forty words per minute, for from forty to forty-five minutes, plunging at once into his theme.

Preaching was exhilarating to him, making him feel as Elihu did—"I will speak that I may be refreshed." Once he preached three hundred times in twelve months. His sermons had many illustrations. Sermonizing involved a great physical strain upon him, but as Beecher said, "he hardened his nerve to it, and made it his normal life."

Though he often preached for "causes," he never omitted the gospel message itself. Always, after he had presented a rousing address at some public gathering upon some topic like "Early Closing," or "Public Penitence," he would say, "Now I cannot make this matter the staple of my discourse"—and off he would go in full flight in gospel truth. Every sermon he preached was an arrow fashioned to create "the slain of Jehovah." He expected conversions. He preached with that compelling unction of a man to whom it was "the first age of Christianity."

He attained the pen of a ready writer in a curious way. Writing was drudgery to him. This was his "literary substitute." On Monday at 7 a. m. the reporter's longhand copy (no typewriters!) of his Sunday sermon was laid before him. This he carefully polished. By Thursday he had the press proofs. These he almost demolished. Copies of his corrected proofs that I have seen look like a printer's nightmare. But in this fashion, though he rarely wrote sermons, he had all the discipline thereof; and developed a forceful style.

It is a surprise to find that he sometimes repeated sermons. He did this in particular on week nights when visiting. On these trips he would very often repeat the sermons he had delivered the previous Sunday. Some of his sermons were many times repeated; as for instance, "The New Song of the Redeemed," which seems to have been his favorite.

His sermons had a tremendous circulation, being translated into many languages and copied by papers all over the world. One man bought 250,000 copies, giving them to every crowned head in Europe, to university students, etc. A single press order was for a million copies. They were published weekly, beginning August 20, 1854, and continuing until 1902, ten years after his death, from "Mss. in store." May I append a few favorites? Livingstone's was "Accidents Not Punishments"; Susannah's, "The Sufferings of Jesus"; to this humble writer heaven seems breathlessly near in "Glory."

Thus far we have simply affirmed what Lord Bacon observed, "Reading maketh a full man." Now we come to the most critical point in a minister's experience–the actual making of a sermon.

First, mark how he got his themes. Here the man was *sui generis*. Listen:

"I very seldom know twenty-four hours beforehand the subject of any sermon I am going to preach!"

He was convinced that each message should be a matter of immediate Guidance. It was sheer presumption for any man to announce subjects a month ahead. And as for a series? Well, the preacher was the determinant in that case and not the Holy Spirit. Therefore, years on end, Saturday afternoon was a sort of open house at Helensburgh or Westwood. At six p. m., however, right after tea, he would say, "Dear friends, good-bye! You know what a number of chickens I have to scratch for." "So with a hearty 'God bless you!' he shook hands with them and shut himself up into companionship with his God" (Susannah). At four o'clock Sunday afternoon he repeated this procedure for the evening sermon. The evening theme was often "simmering in my mind all the morning."

His first step was to wait and watch for the word to be given. This was his most terrible ordeal. He would have God's text for that service, or none at all: "My habit is to look to the Lord for guidance, and when a text comes with power to my soul, I take it without hesitation; but I dare not select my own themes." This made him familiar with the travail of Zion. It was nearly always a terrible ordeal, even from the beginning of his ministry. Here is a sentence from a letter to Susannah before their marriage: "I am down in the valley because I cannot find a subject." The summary of the whole process is found in a late statement of his:

"I confess that I frequently sit hour after hour praying and waiting for a subject, and that is the main part of my study; much hard labor have I spent in manipulating topics, making skeletons out of verses . . . almost every Saturday of my life I prepare enough outlines of sermons to last me for a month, but I no more dare use them than an honest mariner would run ashore a cargo of contraband goods. Let those preach lightly who will; to me it is 'the Burden of the Lord' which at times crushes my whole manhood into the dust of humiliation. I drift on and on over leagues of broken water, till I see the red lights and make sail direct to the desired haven!" He now had a guided text!

When at last he got his text he meditated on it "for my own soul's comfort–not in the professional style of a regular sermon-maker, but feasting upon it for myself! I must know the preciousness of the doctrine in my own experience."

From this point on the "burden" became the "glory." He now called Susannah into the library. Let her tell why. I love to hear her speak:

> "For some time it has been the dear Pastor's custom, as soon as the text has been given him of the Master, to call me into the study and permit me to read the various commentaries on the subject-matter in hand. My heart has burned within me; the marrow and fatness of a precious promise spread like a dainty banquet before my longing eyes. We were both fairly bewildered by the treasures of love and mercy in that fair land of Havilah, where there is gold. I listened to his dear voice condensing the old Puritans in whom he delights. Thus a poor prisoner (she refers to her dreadful, long in-validism) has the first sip of the wine–the first morsel from the loaves with which the thousands are to be fed on the morrow. How shall

I thank God for this holy place in my home where the Lord deigns to draw out my heart in adoration?"

Now let us see what results came from Susannah's reading to him. I quote Spurgeon's own words: "She reads . . . and gradually I am guided as to the best form of outline!" He now had a *guided text* and a *guided outline!* Ah, when a man preaches that way, small wonder that those who listen have their eyes opened for perceiving horses and fire-chariots in the barren mountains of Dothan!

His mind and heart were now full, and God had given him the word. From the vast storehouse of his spirit the garnered treasures were ready to rush forth with the power of Niagara.

Let us stop to note another important characteristic of Spurgeon's preaching; one that could be of incalculable value to our contemporary ministry. *He was never topical, but always textual.* His text was not a mere motto, used as a rubber stamp from Deity to validate his own gossamers. The resources from which he drew were not measured by the strength and store of his own faculties, but by the infinite fulness of the divine Word. In his text he always found his divisions; his sermons were merely an exposition thereof.

This yielded him an amazing result—boundless versatility. He never repeated himself in over 3,500 separate, printed sermons! Newell Dwight Hillis painfully repeated himself every two years, for he was a topical preacher. An index builder for a Spurgeon sermon-set was the first to note this amazing fact; that though he often spoke on the same subject, it was always a unique view thereof, different from whatever he had previously said. Why? Because every text in the Bible has its own, unique, unrepeated and peculiar view of divine truth. When a man selects to be an expository preacher he gains to his sermons the infinite variety of the Book itself. If Spurgeon brings you up again and again to the same old truths, it is always on a different side, or in a new light, or with new surroundings. Let Spurgeon himself sum the case:

"There are hundreds of texts in the Bible which remain like virgin summits, whereon the foot of the preacher has never stood. I might almost say that the major part of the Word of God is in that condition: it is still an Eldorado unexplored, a land whose dust is gold. After thirty-five years I find that the quarry of Holy Scripture is inexhaustible, I seem hardly to have begun to labor in it!"

It would be more than appropriate, in concluding this chapter, as a comment on Spurgeon's sermonizing, to let Charles, one of Spurgeon's sons, describe his father's power:

> "When once father began to speak you felt that each succeeding wave of expression would wash up some new and hitherto hidden truth: while listening to that matchless voice, there seemed to steal over you the low murmur of Another, which told you he was declaring the very oracles of God."

XV

MR. VALIANT-FOR-TRUTH

If you take a wolf in a lambskin, hang him up, for he is the worst of his generation.—*Thomas Adams (1614)*.

That is no Gospel which has not Christ in it; the modern idea of preaching *Truth* instead of Christ is a wicked device of Satan. John Newton put Calvinism into his sermons as he put sugar in his tea. Don't be afraid of putting in an extra lump now and then.—*C. H. S.*

To attempt to be saved by a mixed covenant of faith and works is to yoke a snail with an elephant.—*Berridge (1716-1793)*.

Too many preachers are offended with the stern truths to which the Puritans testified. We are told they need dilution. Any man who does this, does not declare all the counsel of God. The faithful minister must be pointed. He must so preach that his hearers will know whether he preaches a scheme of salvation by works, or salvation by the grace of God.—*C. H. S.*

Mr. Valiant-for-Truth

That interesting chap, Mr. Valiant-for-truth, generally appears in the second episodes of Christian history. This is where John Bunyan put him, in part two of *Pilgrim's Progress.* Bunyan, with Puritan subtlety, observes that Valiant-for-truth's fire came to him at the preaching of Mr. Tell-true, who told of Christian's sufferings, of his gospel and of his triumphant entry into the City Celestial, as recorded in the first book. To use Valiant's own words: "That man so told the story of Christian and his travels that my heart fell into a burning haste to be gone after him; so I got from them, and am come thus far on the way."

Mr. Tell-true in Spurgeon's case was John Calvin; John Calvin's writings and John Calvin's theology as expounded by his admirers in Broad Brims. Calvinism, historically, got firm hold upon Spurgeon in his fifteenth year, April 7, 1850, just between conversion and baptism. That week night he sat in a meeting, thinking but little about the preacher's sermon, for "he did not believe it." The thought struck him, How did you come to be a Christian? Mentally, he followed through the several steps: seeking, conviction, Scripture reading, prayer, regeneration, and perceived God to be at the bottom of it all: "God was the author of my faith. The whole doctrine of grace opened up to me. Those truths were burned into my soul as with a hot iron. I felt

I had grown on a sudden from a babe into a man. From that I have not departed." "That," here, is essentially the essence of Calvinism, even to its five points. Thereafter Calvin and his Puritan interpreters were the Delectable Mountains to Spurgeon. One of the greatest events in his life (to him) was when, at the age of twenty-four, he visited Geneva, wore John Calvin's canonical gown, preached in his pulpit, and was given a Calvin medal by Genevan Christians. He said that when he saw the medal he wept; and kissed it–imagining no one saw the action.

Spurgeon's whole theology thereupon became an ellipse, whose twin foci were substitution and resurrection. Every point revolved in an orderly fashion about these two, all his thinking being consistently clear to him. Time brought development, of course: but change? Never! He boasted continually that the doctrines he began to preach he preached to the end.

Observe what, in the main, these doctrines were. To specify them is not difficult: All men are by nature children of wrath and under judgment; one must not hesitate to sketch terrible pictures of the damned, their misery and despair. But, one must declare positively that Jesus' death on the cross, if accepted, would make a way of escape from judgment for all mankind. And the resurrection proved it. I quote from Spurgeon's writings:

"I have always considered with Luther and Calvin that the sum and substance of the gospel lies in that word substitution–Christ standing in the stead of man. The gospel is this: I deserve to be lost forever; the only reason why I should not be damned is that Christ was punished in my stead, and there is no need to execute a sentence twice for sin.

"I cannot enter heaven without a perfect righteousness: I am absolutely certain I shall never have one of my own. But, then, Christ had a perfect righteousness and he said, 'There, poor sinner, take my garment and put it on; I will suffer in your stead, and you will be rewarded for the works you did not do, but which I did for you.'

"Sink or swim, I go to him; other hope have I none. I find it very convenient every day to come to Christ as a sinner, as I came at the first. The word that drew my soul–'Look unto me'–still rings its clarion note in my ears. There I once found conversion, and there I shall ever find renewal."

He was positive that salvation came in all its entirety through faith, and faith only: "A salvation that does not save outright is neither worth preaching nor worth listening to."

To him no intellectual hiatus appeared between personal responsibility and effectual grace. Both being scriptural, both he preached, and let correlation stand as the business of the Spirit. The Hyper-Calvinists therefore raged against him because he pleaded with men to be reconciled to God; the Arminians sneered when he announced election and the inability of any foreordained man to resist God's call. Evangelistic Calvinism had no phrasal contradictions for him:

"I am as firm a believer in the doctrine of grace

as any man living, and a true Calvinist after the order of John Calvin himself; and probably I have read more of his works than my accusers ever did. *But,* if it be thought to be an evil thing to bid sinners lay hold on eternal life, I will be yet more evil, and herein not only imitate Calvin, but also my Lord, who though he taught salvation is of grace, and grace alone, feared not to speak to men as responsible agents, and bid them enter in at the strait gate."

He even facetiously referred to these apparent contradictions. Once, in Leeds, he read and commented on Romans 9 and 10. Reaching verse 10:13, he said: "Dear me, how wonderfully like John Wesley the apostle talked! 'Whosoever?' Why, that is a Methodist word, is it not?" (Amens from the Methodists; frowns from the Hypers!) "But (he proceeded) read verse 9:11 and see how wonderfully like John Calvin he (Paul) talked—"That the purpose of God according to election might stand.' (Amens and frowns change faces!) The fact is that the whole system of truth is neither here nor there. Be it ours to know what is scriptural in all systems, and accept it."

Yet withal the gospel to him was not complicated, but exceedingly simple: "Two or three plain facts constitute the gospel—'For I delivered unto you first of all that which I also received, how that Christ died for our sins according to the Scriptures; and that he was buried, and that he rose again the third day according to the Scriptures.'"

Such a simple, clear-cut system kept his "point in

the air" at all times against shoddy or shady theology. Songs like "Beautiful Isle of Somewhere" he dismissed as "wax-nose hymnology made to fit any creedal face"; or "mermaid poetry, fair enough where it broke the surface, but altogether fishy in its nether parts." To him songs of this kind were sheer pagan nonsense on the order of "Thanatopsis." These hymns, he suggested, should be turned over to Chief Ojibewas as the liturgical rubric of the Chickasaws, in the worship of the west wind:

> When the wind is blowing,
> Do not shrink or cower,
> Firmly onward going,
> Feel the joy of power.
> Heaviest the heart is
> In the heavy air,
> Every wind that rises,
> Blows away despair.

His views made of him a staunch Baptist, constantly emphasizing the six Baptist distinctives: *the Lordship of Jesus; the Supremacy of the New Testament; Regeneration the basis of church-membership; the Right of private judgment; Separation of civil and religious entities; and Baptism by immersion.* He was absolutely for open communion—"I dare not sit with Baptist alone"—but he was never for open membership—"My church fellowship is entirely of the immersed." To this day he remains an authority on certain early phases of British Baptist history.

His estimates of celebrated contemporaries whose sermons "had no savor of Substitution" were utterly frank. Concerning Henry Ward Beecher he wrote: "Lessons of moral wisdom may be gathered from these sermons, but for sound doctrine we must look elsewhere. As an improvement upon the theology of the Puritan fathers, his teaching will be rejected." The call of the hour to him was for fearless, loyal, Bible preachers, not philosophers: "We want John Knox again; we want fiery John Knox! That which thundered through Scotland must thunder through England again."

Such convictions thrust upon him two great controversies.

In the light of Spurgeon's experience, every man who wishes to be cast in the role of Defender of the Faith should look well to the cost thereof, should inquire diligently about God's will, and never be swayed by seeming glamor. No one can long play that part unless he has a tender heart. For this is the text that must control Mr. Valiant-for-truth: "Speaking the truth in love." Should he fail in this respect he is naught else than Mr. Hard-for-doctrine. But if he *has* a tender heart, he finds it forever bleeding at the sight of wounded friends who come within the circle of his saber-sweeps. Should God himself cast a man in the part, it is to be had a heavy task; but romanticists who rush for the assignment ought to know that it has much more than wound nursing; it means hours of self-doubt, personal misgivings, and fighting when the soul hungers for loving.

John Bunyan, too, knew this. Here is the wording upon Mr. Valiant-for-truth's entry in *Pilgrim's Progress:*

"Just at the place where Little-faith formerly was robbed, there stood a man with his sword drawn, and his face all bloody. Then said Mr. Great-heart, What art thou? The man made answer saying, I am one whose name is Valiant-for-truth. Three men did beset me, to wit, Wild-head, Inconsiderate and Pragmatic (Bunyan forgot to mention Divergent-judgment). They have left upon me, as you see, some of the marks of their valor, and have also carried away with them some of mine."

Bunyan therein neatly summed up Spurgeon's experience. He carried to the grave some of the marks of his adversaries' valor, and just as certainly gave them some of his. Thomas Spurgeon, after his father's death, said to his copastor, Archibald Brown, in reference to a proposition that the Baptist Union hold its coming session in Metropolitan Tabernacle: "The Baptist Union almost killed my father." Brown replied, "Yes, and your father almost killed the Baptist Union."

"It was a tragic experience, leaving Spurgeon at the end of life far more "careful on the draw" than he was in the beginning; chary of saber-rattling. Here are words from his next-to-the-last address:

"During the past year, I have been made to see that there is more love and unity among God's people than is generally believed. I feel myself a debtor to all God's people on earth. We mistake our divergencies of judgment for difference of heart, but they are far from being the same thing."

We present a telegraphic sketch of the two famous controversies.

The baptismal regeneration controversy took place in Spurgeon's thirty-third year (1857); the "Down-Grade" began in his fifty-third year (1887). In the first he contended against Anglicans, who appeared to him as cravens, holding a creed they did not believe. In the second he fought against Nonconformists, who seemed to him cowards, holding a faith which they feared to state. In his mind, these battles were, first on the left wing, against superstition, and then on the right wing, against modernism.

In the first there was a large show of affection for his enemies. He besought God in the famous sermon on baptismal regeneration for a "truly reformed Church of England, and a Godly race to maintain it, the world's future depending upon it." He counted upon sorrow, but it turned out somewhat to his advantage. He had to resign from the Evangelical Alliance of England. He later joined it and a warm friendship grew up between himself and the men against whom he testified. *But*, the Church of England went on in the same old way. W. Y. Fullerton had a melancholy suspicion that the whole affair was a statement of futility.

In the "Down-Grade Controversy" he seems to have had much less kindliness in his attitudes. His opponents were "the adversaries of the Lord"; men who were of orthodox opinion "should not keep company with them; What communion hath Christ with Belial?" He began a barrage of generalities in his monthly magazine, *The Sword and Trowel*, charging certain unnamed Nonconformists with denying the atonement, the resurrection, regeneration and inspiration. Finally, he cast off ambiguity and specified members of the British Baptist Union. This forced his withdrawal from the organization, and the Union passed a vote of censure upon him. He expected sympathy this time, but was disappointed.

In the judgment of many it was a needless sorrow to both sides. Fullerton is sure that had there been a face-to-face conference—even had telephones existed—the whole tragic grief to Spurgeon and his brethren could have been avoided.

Both sides mourned over the broken fellowship. Susannah felt that the controversy cost him his life. To a friend in May, 1891, Spurgeon said, "Good-bye! you will never see me again; this fight is killing me." The thunders, after four years, were beginning to die down. His great heart yearned over his brethren. Among his last utterances was one comparing himself to Garibaldi—"a foreigner in his native land, hoping that those who banish us may be of another mind and enable us to return." His fatal illness began in June, 1891, and while Baptists were busy here and there—*he was gone.*

A Christian Odyssey may be found in the literature and documents of that controversy. One thing rises above it all for those who have open minds—the Sorrows of Werther are small compared with the sorrows of polemics. We would do well to keep from controversy until God himself fills Jeremiah with the intolerable bone-fire of silence. Every protest Spurgeon uttered should have been uttered; yet we have a feeling that something was wrong with our Valiant Galahad in the way he went about it. However, judgments are altogether painful to those of us who love Spurgeon as the greatest single figure since Paul. Personal conclusions, however, are not. Valiant-for-truth must move only in the will of God; and moving, he must never permit his rejoicing to center even in his "Right Jerusalem Blade." Men who take that sword die by it as well as the sword of Mars. The only way Valiant-for-truth may endure at all is for him to carry with his bloody face a heart filled with the compassion of the Young Lord of Glory.

He must also guard rigorously against the anxiety moods of ark supporters, those gratuitous qualms God never asked, nor appreciated; those lapses when "love sinks to anxiety, faith to hope, hope to trembling," and the times appear to be in the last days. Unless Elijah shall always be using his divine correctives, he will fall to the unworthy fear that he alone is left in Israel. Valiant-for-truth may have a bloody face, but we are sure God does not intend him to suffer a broken heart. And Valiant must *think carefully*; it is tragic to find that one has been fighting an ally, Mr. Divergent-opinion, mistaking him for the enemy, Mr. Different-heart.

A most significant, if tragic, figure of the centennial year 1934 is the heroic statue of Spurgeon in the narthex of the London Building of the British Baptist Union; erected by the very men who fought against him; erected by them because of all Baptists he was to them the greatest and best!

XVI

A Puritan Workshop

The towers and bulwarks of Zion are *those doctrines of the true faith,* which are the strength and glory of the church, which are to be maintained in their soundness and stability against the assaults of heretical teachers, so that they may be transmitted unimpaired to following generations - *Theoderet (393-457).*

Encircle Zion again and again with loving perambulations. We cannot too frequently or too deeply consider the origin, privileges, history, security and glory of the church. These are her towers. See how fair are the pleasaunces of "that ancient citie" of which you are citizens. - C. H. S.

A Puritan Workshop

Lord Bacon was once represented as putting one hand on the public schools, the other on state houses, saying, "I gave you these, for I taught you inductive reasoning." We borrow the format. The Puritan could place one hand on the great multitudes that heard Spurgeon, the other on the Metropolitan Tabernacle, and assert, "I made both possible; for I taught you the gospel which drew the crowds, and I showed you the architectural concept best adapted for both the message and the masses." This chapter constitutes, from the standpoint of historical accuracy, the heaviest labor of writing; but it would be hard to point to any other phase of Spurgeon's life having higher value for our contemporary world.

Early in his New Park Street ministry it became obvious that a great house of worship must be erected. Many were convinced that it was folly to think of it. Spurgeon commented tersely on this point. "Build or I resign; either erect the Tabernacle or I become an evangelist." Note that at this early date he said "Tabernacle." That was Puritan influence. He explained: "The word tabernacle involves a religious doctrine. We believe this building to be temporary, meant for the time in the wilderness without the visible King." "Metropolitan" was suggested by the designing architect.

A building committee of thirty was appointed in June, 1856. Lorimer states that "at their first private meeting Spurgeon exclaimed, 'I hear some of you are doubtful; if so, go through that door and stay there.' At a later meeting he repeated the statement. Twelve went out. Said he, 'Any more?' Three more departed, and with seven he marched to victory." This sounds to me like a tall story, though some truth may be in it.

Money started to come in voluntarily. On his twenty-second birthday, June 24,1856, Spurgeon received a small sum by mail: "I wish to be first." This greatly encouraged him. By September $15,000 had come in. On September 29 the building committee held its first public meeting and recommended the building of a Tabernacle to seat 5,000; possible cost, $75,000. It actually did cost nearly $157,000.

The Surrey Hall tragedy soon followed, which may explain why the next public meeting was delayed until March 23, 1857. The cash in hand was now $22,500. Spurgeon began to look for a building lot. He found one that seemed good—a forlorn, vacant piece of ground in Newington Butts, with only the weed-covered wreckage of the ancient Saint Peter's Hospital of the Fishmongers Company. He felt guided that here was the place God wanted.

But there was a wide difference of opinion among New Park Street men as to building lot: "Kensington!" "No,—Holloway!" "Never,—Clapham!" Spurgeon said, "Newington Butts! I have made up my mind not to go elsewhere." The male members— British realestate law—met again September 7 to settle the matter. It was settled before the meeting began. Every man who had a wife, daughter, sister or sweetheart had this injunction before he left home: "Never mind what anybody else says; vote what your pastor proposes."

Spurgeon argued it was holy associations of the past that influenced him in favor of Newington Butts: "Baptists were burned right there. The blood of the martyrs is the seed of the church. Besides, right there many great London highways converge." The vote was so emphatic that opposition died. Petticoat lobby carried the day!

On the news of purchase, money started to come in a torrent—$1,700 a month. A freehold site was obtained in December at a cost of $25,000—"on which to erect our holy and beautiful house" leaving a treasury balance of $18,000. Immediately on purchase $5,000 more came in.

The committee now publicly advertised for plans. The directions contained this amazing sentence, "Gothic designs will not be accepted." Why? Spurgeon didn't want Gothic. Why? Puritan ideals. He said:

"I look at a building from a theological point of view, not from an architectural. There are two sacred languages in the world . . . Hebrew of old . . . the other is not Rome's mongrel tongue, Latin; . . it is Greek! I care not how many an idol temple has been built after this fashion . . . the standard of our faith is Greek, and this place is to be Grecian. We owe nothing to the Goths as religionists. Every Baptist place should be Grecian, not Gothic."

That was of the very essence of Puritanism; for its architectural concept declares war on the Gothic.

The Puritans felt that vaulted nave and pointed arch were the enemies of New Testament vigor. Formality might be served in dim religious lights, but evangelism could do naught else than sicken and die in such atmosphere. They were sure that recording angels in the department of ecclesiastical architecture wept when they saw blueprints providing Cologne cathedrals for churches of the Congregational type. A. T. Pierson declared that "Spurgeon was right; a building, plain, large, and free, built without regard to display, and evidently intended for the multitudes, strangely attracts the multitudes."

By February, 1859, sixty-two separate plans and one model were submitted by architects. E. C. Robbins was awarded first prize. Spurgeon felt W. W. Pocock's was the best; so did the committee. Pocock's plan had four elaborate towers at the corners, costing $5,000 each. Spurgeon said, "Mere show. Take them off. I'll have no ornament that has no practical value"—that sounds like Charnock. Someone replied, "You can't leave them off; the roof looks too high without them." Spurgeon rejoined, "Those who look at the Tabernacle from the outside have not subscribed; they cannot judge its true beauty." The towers came off.

William Higgs got the contract at $107,500. Operations began. One night while the grounds were covered with bricks and lumber, Spurgeon and Deacon Cook, secretary of the building committee, knelt and prayed God's blessing on the building enterprise. The corner-stone was laid August 16,

1869. The money on hand was far short of the needs. But they moved forward.

Spurgeon said, "No debt! We'll go no further than the funds." (Remember the slate-pencil story?) "We'll put up the carcass, roof it in, allow the people to stand. Those who want seats can buy them." Twenty-five thousand dollars in new subscriptions were laid on the corner-stone that day.

In all this it will be observed that his executive instincts were exceedingly prominent. When calling an associate pastor, the church wrote into the call the condition that he must agree to resign on twelve months' notice, or immediately upon payment of one year's stipend—should Spurgeon desire it. When Spurgeon found a member who differed offensively from the church's basis of agreement in doctrine and practice, he simply said to that person, "Please withdraw from the church"—and that was *that!* Publicly he stated, "I am captain of this vessel. If there should be a Jonah in this ship, I shall in as Christian a spirit as possible pitch him out. I shall not think that because Jonah is there I ought to leave, but I will stand by the ship in all weather as well as in sunshine." Knights of the Unsustained Surrender, however, will do well to refrain from copying. There is a story of an evil spirit who said to his would-be exorcists, "Jesus I know, and Paul I know; but who are ye?"

Money poured in from all over the world. Humanity and God are fond of faith projects. By April 2, 1860, the total receipts were $94,250. Sixty thousand dollars more was needed. Spurgeon said, "No debt! We'll not go in till it's paid for." Operations continued on practically a cash basis.

On January 6, 1861, they still lacked twenty thousand dollars. The building was nearing completion; plans were being made for dedication. Spurgeon kept insisting, "No debt; we will not dedicate till the money is provided." April 1, 1861, was provisionally set as the date of dedication. The third day before Spurgeon announced, "The whole sum has been given, and we will enter free from debt next Sunday."

A million people representing all classes had subscribed. John Ruskin gave five hundred dollars. Spurgeon himself brought in from outside preaching trips over twenty thousand dollars. The church immediately began a five weeks' revival in the new building. When building operations started in 1856 they had fifteen hundred members; by May, 1861, there were twenty-five hundred.

With all this herculean task in progress, the church kept up its missionary activities unabated, starting new missions and financing them. While the Tabernacle was being builded they did as much as any other church for outside causes.

In this vast enterprise of faith Spurgeon moved with unfaltering assurance. His faith was lifted to a high plane by a stranger who put one hundred thousand dollars in bonds and leases in his hands, to "fall back on" if needed. Spurgeon resolved this money should never be used; and it wasn't. "But I had no excuse for fear." To *all* of this miracle of

An Interior View

Exterior

Metropolitan Tabernacle

finance we add the radiant comment, "Where God guides, he provides."

The building was imposing in its simple beauty, and of honest structure all the way through. Spurgeon hated sham in architecture, once quoting this verse:

> They build the front just like St. Marks,
> Or like Westminster Abbey;
> And then, as if to cheat the Lord,
> They make the back part shabby.

The structure, with auxiliary rooms, was 174 feet over all. The auditorium proper had 25,225 feet of floor space, was 146 feet long, 81 feet wide, with an elliptical ceiling, 62 feet above main floor level.

The auditorium floor level was some ten feet above ground level, gained by outside steps. This made possible, by half-basement effects, quarters for Bible school, prayer-meeting, etc. The actual seating capacity was forty-six hundred—all free seats. The pulpit platform took off from the first gallery (there were two) fifteen feet above the main floor. Four feet above the main floor level (just beneath the pulpit), was a small platform into which the baptistry was sunk. Pulpit and baptistry thus made a sort of two-story arrangement, the pulpit above the baptistry, and both in full view of every seat. Several vestries led off from the auditorium.

There was no organ; all singing was a capella, led by a precentor. Spurgeon said, "Services of religion will be conducted without any peculiarity or innovation. No musical or aesthetic accompaniment will ever be used." His views on church music would be intolerable today; that is, Spurgeon's views, *without* Spurgeon. Get the tension of this: "What a degradation to supplant the intelligent song of the whole congregation by the theatrical prettiness of a quartette, the refined niceties of a choir, or the blowing off of wind from inanimate bellows and pipes. We might as well pray by machinery as praise by it." Here he made even the Puritans appear liberals; for did not George Swinnock (1627-1673)–he of the close-pressed lips–say: "When many skilful musickians play in concert with well-timed and prepared instruments, the musick cannot be but ravishing to God Himself!" Yet for over thirty years that building was packed several times a week. Which makes us feel sure that the crowds that poured out of Jerusalem to hear John the Baptist did not go to study his diet, or to copy styles from his walking-suit.

The descriptions of the average Sunday service at Metropolitan, printed in the world's newspapers for years, are so interestingly alike that we submit a single average account:

> "Arrived half-hour ahead; crowd already there. Refused admission at one of the fifteen doors–'Must have ticket.' Ticket secured. Admitted. Building well filled. Doors opened to public when big clock points to 10.55. Crowd surges in filling every available space. At 11.00, sharp, in comes a plain man, Spurgeon, followed by some dozen deacons. He prays; we all sing;

wonderful! Scripture. We all sing again. He prays (wonderful). He preaches–melodious voice, Anglo-Saxon words, soul-stirring message. We all sing again. Final prayer–and we go back to our quarters feeling we've had a foretaste of heaven!"

This was "the Tabernacle average" for thirty-seven years; and then?

No more appropriate end could be imagined than what did take place. When the great preacher died his work was ended, and with it the need for its visible machinery. In an interview with W. T. Stead, June, 1884, Spurgeon disclosed his inner feeling on the subject. Here are sentences from that statement:

"Whenever anything is to be done, depend upon it, it is done by one man. The whole history of the church teaches this. A Moses, a Gideon . . . are from time to time raised up . . . when they pass away, their work appears to cease. . . . Hence I am against all endowments for religion. . . Let each generation provide for its own wants. . . One great object of every religious teacher should be to prevent the creation of external appliances to make his teaching appear to live, when it is dead."

Spurgeon died January 31, 1892; and then–the Tabernacle burned to the ground, April 20, 1898!

A new church building was completed in 1900, considerably smaller in capacity. *And it has an organ!*

XVII

Life-Changer

The property of a Christian is, *fides per delectionem efficax*, faith worked by love. What availeth it to pretend faith toward God, where there is no love toward thy neighbor? And wherein can thy love be declared more than in this, to draw thy neighbor to the participation of that same merit whereunto God hath called thee? Since the Lord hath put out his merciful hand to draw us out of the prison of sin, shall we refuse to put out our hand to draw up our brethren with us?–*William Cowper (1566-1619).*

The capacity of acting upon individuals is now almost a lost art. It is hard to learn again. We have spoiled ourselves by thinking to draw thousands by public work–by what people call "pulpit eloquence." We have been painting Madonnas and Ecce Homos and choirs of angels, like Raphael, and it is hard to condescend to the beggar boy of Murillo. We have forgotten the simple way of the Founder–how He ran away from cities, how He lagged behind the rest at Samaria to have a quiet talk with *one woman* at a well . . . In small groups of two's and three's He collected the early church around Him. One by one the disciples were called–and there were only twelve in all.–*Henry Drummond, "The New Evangelism and Other Essays."*

One result of months of study of the memorabilia of Spurgeon's life is, increasing astonishment at the great amount of time he spent in personal evangelism. It is easy to think of him before vast congregations, moving men's hearts with his golden voice and honest thinking. In this fashion a thousand writers have pictured him. There was another Spurgeon, exercising a yet nobler art than sacred oratory; the Spurgeon who spent a long time with a single coster-monger in Newington Butts, one humble boy at the Orphanage, one forgotten bobby, walking his beat in the slums. That heated soul of his, toward which thousands turned for comfort, came to its warmth in the same way as did the soul of Another, who, from the exhilaration of dealing with *one woman* at a well, uttered those significant words, "I have meat to eat that ye know not of." We are coming to understand better than men used to the mystery of Spurgeon's power. It was a mistake to seek his assay through pulpit-ore samples alone. We now perceive that his uncanny knowledge of the human heart and his wonderful skill in moving multitudes may be attributed largely to the hours he spent in the clinic of his personal intercourse with people.

Fascinating it is beyond words, to watch Spurgeon's example in personal work inflame first the imagination of Dwight L. Moody; then watch Henry Drummond "get his eyes open" in Moody's inquiry room; and, finally, in 1873, to behold Drummond writing his essay on *Spiritual Diagnosis,* which "marked the beginning of the modern movement of scientific evangelism, if not the psychology of religion as well."[1] It is an unbroken glow through Drummond to Moody, Moody to Spurgeon, Spurgeon to the Puritans, and from the Puritans to Pentecost.

Research shows this man under the Broad Brim to have mastered the vital New Testament soul-saving approach long before our ears ever heard such challenging phrases as "Life-changing on a colossal scale." His work as a life-changer began the next day after his own conversion. We quote from a letter to his mother, dated June 11, 1850:

"Dear Mother:

"Truly, indeed, I have much for which to bless the Lord, when I contemplate his Divine Sovereignty, and see that my salvation is entirely of his free electing love. I have more than sufficient to induce me to give up myself entirely to him who has bought me and purchased me with an everlasting redemption.

I have seventy people whom I regularly visit on Saturday. I do not give a tract and go away; but I sit down and endeavor to draw their attention to spiritual realities. I have great reason to believe the Lord is working—the people are so kind and pleased to see me."

This distribution of little printed pages as an approach to interviews was a distinctive Puritan

[1] H. A. Walter, Soul Surgery.

device; they fairly snowed England down with tracts in the sixteenth century.

His first convert gave him "such rejoicing as one that findeth great spoil." He wrote: "If anybody said to me, 'Someone has left you twenty thousand pounds,' I should not have given a snap of my fingers for it, compared with the joy I felt when I was told God had saved a soul through my ministry." Early of a Monday morning he had a deacon drive him to the village where she lived, a poor laboring man's wife. He dealt with her personally. Later, in prayer, he sobbed out his Te Deum, "Oh God, this is thy first seal to my ministry! Thou knowest I would rather be the means of saving her soul from death than to be the greatest orator on earth!"

Which probably is the precise explanation of his becoming one of the world's greatest preachers. Schindler quotes Cornelius Elven's analysis of Spurgeon's eloquence: "He told anecdotes of the usefulness of addressing individuals one by one about their souls." Schindler also quotes John B. Gough as saying: "I have seen Mr. Spurgeon holding by his power sixty-five hundred people in breathless interest; but as he sat by the bedside of a dying child whom his beneficence had rescued he was to me a greater and grander man than when swaying the mighty multitude at his will."

It is a distinct loss that most writers have overshadowed Spurgeon the life-changer by Spurgeon the preacher–too many thousands of clergymen have thus set to imitating the wrong end of his example. A certain Roman soldier, who paid a great price to get what came to Paul by birthright, made the discovery that even then, he was a "factitious citizen" while Paul was a "natural." Underwriting Spurgeon's golden oratory was his capacity for acting on individuals, and any clergyman who aims at pulpit power in any other way will but get himself the sound of cymbals and the clang of brass. This acting on individuals with Spurgeon followed every kind of outlet. His life-changing letters, in his own hand, are a revelation. He was always at the business of gathering unto himself a race of Timothys: "When *you* are gone out into the vineyard, I must find another to be my dearly beloved Timothy, just as you are" (letter to T. W. Medford). When Spurgeon died, he had personally drilled an army of nine hundred of the sons of Eunice!

We pause to give details as to the number of hours he spent in life-changing:

"From the very early days of my ministry in London, the Lord gave me such an abundant blessing upon the proclamation of his truth that, whenever I was able to appoint a time for seeing converts and inquirers, it was seldom that I waited in vain. On one occasion I had a very singular experience, which enabled me to realize the meaning of our Lord's answer to his disciples' question . . . 'Jesus saith, my meat is to do the will of him that sent me.' Leaving home early one morning, I went to the Chapel and sat there all day long. . . I may have seen some thirty or more persons during the day, one after another; I was so delighted that I did not know anything about how the time passed. A little before ten o'clock (p. m.) I felt faint; and I began to think at what hour I had my dinner . . . I had not had any! I never thought of it, I never even felt hungry, because God had made me . . . so satisfied with Divine manna, the heavenly food of success in winning souls."

Susannah said that this kind of activity went on year after year: "Tuesday afternoons with rare exceptions, he gave himself to the truly pastoral and important work of seeing inquirers at the Tabernacle; and in no part of his service was Mr. Spurgeon more happy." Charles, Junior, wrote after his father's death: "Father liked me to go out driving with him; he would tell of recent instances. In this way I learned much of the holy art of dealing with anxious inquirers, an art of which he was indeed a master."

"Sharing" is a familiar term in the religious vocabulary of today. Samuel J. Shoemaker, Jr., defines it: "I try to share with them whatever part of my own life bears most directly upon them and their situation." Of course the Young Galilean said this and said it better in his words, "Go to thy house, unto thy friends, and tell them what great things the Lord hath done for thee." This so-called "sharing" is God's chosen way, leagues and leagues ahead of mere theologizing and argumentation. It was Spurgeon's main approach in life-changing. I quote him:

"Very often, when inquirers have come to me they have told their tale with an air of the greatest possible wonder, and asked me whether it was not extremely unusual . . . 'Now sit down,' I say, 'and I will tell you what were my feelings.' . . . 'Why, sir,' he exclaims, 'that is just how I have felt; but I did not think anyone else had ever gone over the same path I had trodden.' It is no wonder that, when we have little acquaintance with each other's spiritual experience, our way should seem a solitary one; but he who knows much of the dealings of God with poor, seeking sinners, is well aware that their experiences are, in the main, very much alike.

"I know that a man's own experience is one of the very best weapons he can use in fighting with evil in other men's lives. Often, their misery and despondency, aggravated, as it commonly is, by a feeling of solitariness, will be greatly relieved before it is effectually driven out, when they find that a brother has suffered the same, and yet has been able to overcome. Do I show how precious the Saviour is to my soul? . . Right soon will he look into the same dear face and be lightened."

Here is a lovely little story from Susannah's lips, characteristic of her Tirshatha's life-changing labors. After Spurgeon's death an ex-policeman, an old man named Coleman, completely bedridden, never tired of telling his memories of the early days, when the world flocked to hear "the boy preacher": "Oh, he was a dear, good young man, he did not make himself anything! he would shake hands with anyone, he would give me such a grip. He did look pleased, that Sunday morning, when he said, 'Coleman, what do you think? God has blessed me with two little sons!' I used to go in and sit just inside the door, and get a feast for my soul from his discourses. I shall see him again soon, I hope!"

XVIII

GIANT DESPAIR

Think of *this*, ye that feel the heaviness of your soul; Know there is a sorrow "that worketh repentance not to be repented of." Know again there is a sorrow "that worketh death." Remember there are tears that got sinful Mary into heaven; remember again there are tears that got sinful Esau *nothing* . . . If the former be the ground of thy sorrows, know, that thy Saviour hath already blessed thee. The angels are thy servants, they gather thy tears; God is thy treasurer, He lays them up in His bottle; the Holy Ghost is thy comforter, He will not leave thee. Fear not then, to be thus cast down, fear not to be thus disquieted within thee.–*Brian Duppa (1588-1662), "The Soule's Soliloquie."*

Trapp says "David chideth David out of the dumps." Why this depression, why this chicken-hearted melancholy? If I cannot keep a public Sabbath, yet wherefore do I deny my soul her indoor Sabbath? The causes are not enough to justify yielding to despondency. Up, my heart! Play the man, and thy castings down shall turn to liftings up. "Hope thou in God." Hope carries stars in her eyes. Her light is fed by secret visitation from God. . . Let us fly to our God! Blessed downcastings that drive us to Thee, O Lord.–C. H. S.

Giant Despair

There was one aspect of Spurgeon's life, glossed over by most of his biographers, that we must now view with utter frankness—he was frequently in the grip of terrific depression moods. This offers no difficulty whatever to any Christian who does sometimes himself walk the floor of hell, on and on, until he finds a Hand that brings him out. The sweetness of his release giveth him such radiant new love for his Redeemer, that he doth then find in his head the tongue of the taught, enabling him to sustain with words any other that may be weary. The function of "word sustention" is the chief part of Christian ministry. That Saint of Neuritis, Dr. J. H. Jowett, said, "The world wants to be comforted." *He knew that;* and he knew wondrously well how it is done. The tongue of the taught belongs only to those who also are men of sorrows and acquainted with grief.

The Young King had no better engines to make of Spurgeon a polished shaft, in whom He would be glorified, than Spurgeon's fathomless misgivings and the circumstances that provoked them. His song was thrilling to human ears because he came near to the throne out of great tribulation. Here we find the secret of his surpassing humility; and of the fact that a whole world, from sailors on the ships of the Seven Seas to lords of castles, was expectantly eager to read the current week's sermon from the Metropolitan Pulpit.

The Dreamer of Bedford put the entire case into the episode of Giant Despair. Christian pulled the key of Promise out of his bosom and began to try the dungeon door, in whose "nasty and stinking cell" he so long had lain. Lo, the bolts gave back, one after another, though "some went damnably hard," until he was safe again on the King's Highway. Then he did erect a finger-post at the place where he went off, warning others with such good effect, that they escaped the danger.

Spurgeon's depression moods arose from a number of circumstances. For one thing, his whole life, from early teens, was a record of recurrent physical anguish. "April 6, 1850–Heard Mr. S. from Genesis 12:8; could not take it to heart, headache would not let me" (*Secret Diary*), "The first Sunday after his illness, he was almost carried up the pulpit stairs" (contemporary account of Surrey Hall meetings, 1857). We quote a typical account of his trials from a letter of his dated from Mentone, January 10, 1884:

"I am altogether stranded. I am not able to leave my bed, or to find much rest upon it. The pains of rheumatism, lumbago and sciatica, mingled together, are exceedingly sharp. I am aware I am dwelling in a body capable of the most acute suffering." An excerpt from another letter, to Susannah, reads: "After the deadly chill of Thursday night at Nice, I feel gout coming on. . . . My left foot is badly swollen, and the knee joint is following suit. I have had very little sleep, and am very low." A letter to Archibald Brown, dated from the Nightingale

Lane house, about 1869, says, "I thank you for preaching for me. . . . I am better, but have had a sharp nip. Lucian says, 'I thought a cobra had bitten me and filled my veins with poison; but it was worse–*it was gout.*' That was written from experience, *I know.*"

The storm of affliction broke into a steady roar after his forty-third year, necessitating his making almost twenty fall-winter trips to the sunshine of Mentone, France. This took him out of his pulpit two or three of the most valuable months of the year. Under such constraint his spirit chafed: "We *could* do more, we *would* do more, if we were not laid prostrate at the very moment our work requires our presence. Therefore, while we live, every interval of relief shall be laid out in his service. The time is short, the work is great, the Lord must be trusted more simply." Once his depression grew to such size, that he intimated resigning. But his officiary said, "We would rather have you one month in the year than any other twelve."

It is unnecessary to furnish a clinical history; these specimens average his life. There were other factors producing depression; financial worry one of them. It might appear singular after what has been said of Spurgeon's faith financing to find him with money worries. But he had them; and is thereby endeared to those of us who try to follow him with unequal steps. The very giant size of his institutions sometimes overwhelmed him, especially when he was sick. He gives us full details: "During a very serious illness, I had an unaccountable fit of anxiety about money matters. One of the brethren, after trying to comfort me, went straight home, and came back to me bringing all the stocks and shares and deeds and available funds he had, putting them down on the bed; 'There, dear Pastor, I owe everything I have in the world to you, and you are quite welcome to all I possess.' Of course I soon got better and returned it all to my dear friend." It comforts us greatly to know that Spurgeon, in church finance, had constantly to strengthen himself in God.

Still another burden was the Surrey Hall tragedy (see Chapter XI). He never fully recovered from it. At any time of extreme pain, he relived in terrible vividness the whole ghastly scene. It was apt to arise, like Banquo's ghost, at any festival. Once while he was crossing the Alps, at Col di Val Dobbia, a baggage mule lost its footing and glissaded down the slope. It didn't go over the edge; stopped short on the rim and was rescued. But Spurgeon promptly sat down in the snow at that eight thousand foot level and would not, could not, for a long time be persuaded to move. Susannah said, "We coaxed and pleaded to no purpose; so we sat down with him in the snow . . . that awful night at Surrey Hall was responsible . . . the delicate organism of his wonderful brain had then sustained so much pressure, in some part of it, that any sudden fright would have power for a moment or two to disturb its balance."

Then there was the "Down Grade" which gave him months of despondence—but why go further?

We sum it all up in saying that from boyhood days dreadful moods of depression repeatedly tormented Spurgeon. Every mental and spiritual labor at such times had to be carried on under protest of spirit. "The chariot wheels drag heavily," he often sighed. "Even prayer seems like labor; the chariot wheels drag heavily; yet they are not taken off."

Let no one mistake the object of this chapter; it is not a brief of handicaps; it is an explanation of power. "Out of Egypt have I called my Son." Spurgeon came through fire and water into his large place. The grand result with him of every such Mara was a fresh Elim. Bunyan knew what he was about when he set the Delectable Mountains as the next stop after the Castle of Giant Despair.

By means of these tragic hours Spurgeon's reliance was kept on God and not on himself. He finally came to the place where he was sure a great blessing was about to break when Depression stormed his soul: "Depression comes over me whenever the Lord is preparing a larger blessing for my ministry. It has now become to me a prophet in rough clothing. A John the Baptist, heralding the nearer coming of my Lord's richer benison."

Often enough he found that richer benison to be a deepened confidence in the sufficiency of grace. Did he not first discover that mighty truth in one of the darkest hours of his early months in London? Scarcely had he been pastor of New Park Street twelve months when Asiatic cholera swept like shellfire through the tenement section around the chapel. He gave every ounce of youthful ardor to visiting the sick and dying. But he watched his friends fall one by one, until "a little more work and weeping would have laid me low among the rest." Giant Despair had seized him.

One day, returning from a funeral, ready to sink under the burden, his curiosity led him to read a paper wafered up in a shoemaker's window. In bold handwriting were these words, "Because thou hast made the Lord, which is my refuge, even the Most High, thy habitation, there shall no evil befall thee, neither shall any plague come nigh thy dwelling." He said, "The effect was immediate. I felt secure, refreshed, girt with immortality. I went on with my visitation of the dying in a calm and peaceful spirit."

His satisfaction in seeing the travail of his soul may be summed up in a sentence: He blessed God that his fearful experiences prepared him to sympathize with others, to guide them. "I would go into the deeps a hundred times to cheer a downcast spirit. It is good for me to have been afflicted, that I might know how to speak a word in season to one that is weary."

Lacordaire wrote a lucid summary of the economy of suffering in the lives of God's servants: "Moreover, it is with the orator as with Mount Horeb, before God strikes him, he is but a barren rock, but as soon as the divine hand has touched him, as it were with a finger, there burst forth streams that water the desert."

Here is a specimen showing how Spurgeon was able to comfort others with the same comfort whereby he was comforted. From Montreal came this rewarding letter:

> "Oh, Mr. Spurgeon, that little word of yours, 'I am feeling low,' struck a chord which still vibrates in my spirit. It was to me like reading the Forty-second Psalm. I imagine there is nothing in your ministry to the saints that comes home more tenderly to tried and stricken souls than just what you there express, 'I am feeling low.' The great preacher, the author of *The Treasury of David*, this man sometimes, aye, often, 'feels low' just as they do. In all their affliction he was afflicted–this is what draws hearts to Jesus; and the principle is just the same when the friends and intimates of Jesus 'feel low.' The fellow feeling, thus begotten, makes many wondrous kind.
>
> "Your friend in Jesus,
>
> "JOHN LOUSON."

XIX

By-Products

The Septuagint calls mighty men "the sons of rams." These bell-wethers should not cast their crest the higher, because the shepherd hath bestowed a bell upon them, more than upon the rest of the flock.–*John Trapp (1669).*

We have plenty of people nowadays who could not kill a mouse without publishing it in the *Gospel Gazette*. Samson killed a lion and said nothing about it: the Holy Spirit finds modesty so rare that He takes care to record it. Say much of what the Lord has done for you, but say little of what you have done for the Lord. Do not utter a self-glorifying sentence!–*C. H. S.*

The numerous incidentals of Spurgeon's ministry were of such colossal mold as to make him a biographer's despair. In my library there is a shelf of Lives whose authors got so badly confused by the intaglio details of his side-lines that they failed to present his full-length portrait. The artist's time ran out while he was still sketching the brocade on the prince's waistcoat. We insist, therefore, in shutting those vigorous giants, begotten of Spurgeon's genius, into the narrow precincts of a single chapter. Here we propose to keep them, lest in admiring their Talus-like strides we neglect their genitor. It is our aim to set forth chiefly the dynamic faith of the man who called them into being; so that imitation may follow Spurgeon's spirit, not his mechanics. We employ the device of certain architectural reporters, who sketch their buildings as a sum of blurred masses; then as an inset give a detailed bit of frieze bearing the legend, "This treatment goes entirely around the building." Why not? Detail has always been the arch enemy of a unity concept.

There were the books of which he was the author. One hundred and thirty-five in all, with twenty-eight others which he edited, making, with albums and pamphlets, the unbelievable total of more than two hundred! How long would this modern world wait for a review of that forty-foot shelf?

No; these tomes shall be observed *en masse*, with but a few sentences of detail. Seventy-five were distinctly sermonic, bearing over three thousand separate sermons. No one today has even read them all.

Pick out a few notable volumes. *John Ploughman's* Talks. Spurgeon's background hero was Will Richardson, a godly ploughman of Stambourne. When Charles was a boy he tagged along in the furrows after Will, drinking in the man's homely, quaintly beautiful spiritual philosophy; then he gave him immortality; for this book is sure to live in English literature. *The Treasury of David;* seven volumes on the Psalms; twenty years in preparation; the British Museum ransacked for materials; the largest available body of Puritan divinity in the world today outside the William Jewell College collection; a work so excellent that J. H. Jowett said, "Not eclipsed even when set in the radiant succession of Calvin and Luther and Paul." *The Saint and His Saviour,* published by Skinflints in 1857. The copyright is worth ten thousand dollars, but the publishers gave Spurgeon only two hundred. (He didn't make that mistake again.) *Morning by Morning, Evening by Evening* and *The Cheque Book of Faith.* Radiant devotional volumes, the last being Spurgeon's own faith sanctions during the "Down Grade." *Feathers for Arrows—*jolly good sermon illustrations. Two volumes of *Lectures to My Students.* Read these and see where many of the Yale Lecturers on preaching get their materials! *Commentating and Commentators—*not yet out of date. The *Gospel and the Kingdom—*his last book, an exposition of Matthew. *The Clue to the Maze*, his tiniest book; *The Interpreter*, his largest.

That's enough. Think! This mass of books produced by a man who felt that writing is the work of a slave! On the completion of his first book, *The Saint and His Saviour*, he foresaw his prolific literary future: "Nothing but a sense of duty has impelled me to finish this little book, which has been more than two years on hand. Yet have I, at times, so enjoyed the meditation which my writing has induced that I would not discontinue the labor were it ten times more irksome; and moreover, I have some hopes that it may yet be a pleasure to me to serve God with my pen as well as the life."

Dr. John Campbell published a gentle rebuke to the "half-baked youngster": "Such hopes are innocent; it will be wise if Mr. Spurgeon moderates his expectation. The number who attain eminence both with tongue and pen is small. The Greeks produced none; the Romans one; Great Britain hardly more successful. It is Mr. Spurgeon's wisdom to know his place, and be satisfied to occupy it." Mr. Spurgeon's rebuttal was an average of over four books a year for the next thirty-five years!

The monthly paper, *The Sword and Trowel*, began in 1865. It was designed primarily to promote financial aid for Spurgeon's enterprises. But it was packed full of interesting material, largely autobiographical. It is a treasure. In copies I have seen, the book reviews and editorials make about the raciest, sauciest reading anywhere to be found, and cause Bernard Shaw to appear a neophite. And

John Ploughman's Almanac, issued annually from 1874—well, further inventory is an intolerable burden.

Spurgeon wrote no small amount of poetry. For the most part it makes us think of a review in an 1882 issue of *The Sword and Trowel* in which he quotes a San Francisco paper as saying, "During some recent excavations in Assyria a poem on 'The Silver Moon' was dug up. It was engraved on a tile, and close beside it were lying a club and part of a human skull. You may draw your own conclusions!"

However, some of his poems have a certain excellence. "Immanuel," written at eighteen, has an exalted devotional spirit. One inscribed to Susannah is altogether a worthy sentiment of love between husband and wife. The following is one of the few having real excellence:

> What the hand is to the lute,
> What the breath is to the flute,
> What is fragrance to the smell,
> What the spring is to the well,
> What the flower is to the bee,
> That is Jesus Christ to me.
>
> What's the mother to the child,
> What the guide in pathless wild,
> What is oil to troubled wave,
> What is ransom to the slave,
> What is water to the sea,
> That is Jesus Christ to me.

There should follow a briefer notice of Spurgeon as a lecturer. Incredible that he should have time for it, but he did. Here are some of his subjects: "The Two Wesleys"; "Counterfeits"; "Lord Mayors of London"; "Bats, Moles and Hedgehogs"; "Seraphic Zeal-George Whitefield"; "Poland"; "George Fox"; "Candles"; "Miracles of Modern Times."

Then there were the auxiliary organizations of Metropolitan Tabernacle. Who has the courage today closely to study the forty-nine mission Bible schools, which together with the main school had a total enrolment-as run on my office adding-machine-of 7,887 pupils, with 687 officers and teachers? And what thanks would 1934 accord this book for any detailing of lusty secondaries such as these?

The Christian Brothers Benefit Society; The Evangelists' Association and Country Mission; The Flower Mission; The Gospel Temperance Society; The Ladies' Benevolent Society; The Ladies' Maternal Society; The Tract Loan Society; The Tract Society; The Poor Ministers' Clothing Society; The Ragged Schools; The Day Schools; The Society of Evangelists; The Missionary College Association; The Pioneer Work; The Lay Preachers (130 of them in the year 1890); The Colportage Association (founded September 3, 1866, with ninety-six workers; selling in one year nearly twenty thousand Bibles), etc.

Think of one man acting as nerve center for such a race of giants, acting in many cases as treasurer -bemoaning the "Haddon" in his name when he wrote the hundreds of checks-and attending most of their annual meetings-listening to their annual reports of so many sheets, blankets, pillow-cases and other garments distributed. Nearly every week in the year occurred the anniversary of some one of these organizations. Susannah said, "There never was a busier life than his; not an atom more of sacred service could have been crowded into it."

Herewith I supply three insets of vignette detail: for the balance, "This treatment goes entirely around the building."

First and foremost, a résumé of Spurgeon's plan of financing his institutions. George Müller was frankly his inspiration. In 1867 Spurgeon publicly said, "I hope the day may soon come when the noble example which has been set by our esteemed brother, Mr. Müller of Bristol, will be more constantly followed in all the Lord's work."

That example was faith-financing. It is leagues ahead of the modern plan of calling in the high-pressure corporation to "put on a drive." Some of us know that whole deadly process all too well–hip-hurrah sales talks, long-term pledges, "fully subscribed," debts incurred, pledges begin to shrink, embarrassment, despair and spiritual headache for years to come! If only heaven could deputize Spurgeon for one year's general work in the world, to reveal the ease, joy and blessedness of faith-financing, then the high-pressure boys would need seek other jobs.

Spurgeon did not even permit solicitors to take pledges. The need was simply and frankly stated in the pulpit and then in *The Sword and Trowel;*

this was followed by intercessory prayer to find God's will and secure his resources—and the gold flood poured in. Here is his entire policy in his own words:

"It was this way in the building of this Tabernacle. We were a few and poor people when we commenced; but, still, we moved on by faith, and never went into debt. . . We trusted in God. And mark you, it will be so in the erection of this Orphan Home . . . *Our faith will precede our sight.* But if we go on the old custom . . . get our subscribers, and send around our collectors, and pay our percentages,—that is, do not trust God, but trust our subscribers—if we go by that rule, we shall see very little, and have no room for believing. But if we shall just trust God, and believe that he never did leave a work that he put upon us, and never set us to do a thing without meaning to help us through with it, we shall soon see that the God of Israel still lives, and that his arm is not shortened."

Here is how the Stockwell Orphanage came into being: At a Monday evening prayer-service, in 1866, Spurgeon said: "We are now a huge church, and should be doing more for our Lord in this great city. Let's ask him to send us some new work; and if we need money to carry it on, let's pray that the means also may be sent." Within a few days, Mrs. Anne Hillyard, widow of an Episcopalian clergyman and a reader of *The Sword and Trowel,* designated one hundred thousand dollars to Spurgeon, specifying that it should be used to found an orphanage. Susannah notes, "Here was the new work, and the money with which to begin it; it came from the Lord in answer to the petitions offered that Monday night. Surely the orphanage was born of prayer."

In January, 1867, two and one-half acres in Stockwell were optioned. Then came a financial panic. Mrs. Hillyard's money was in railroad debentures, which promptly "froze up." Spurgeon again affirmed the faith-financing policy—no debt, no hypothecation of frozen assets. The first four orphans were quartered in a private home. To provide their expenses, Mrs. Hillyard sold her plate.

Gifts began to pour in by the thousands; ground was purchased; the foundation stone set August 9, 1867—twelve thousand dollars was laid on the stone. Dramatic prayer-answers came like a mystery tale. Once the treasury was empty, and cash was needed for the contractor, in two days; prayer; then an unknown giver sent five thousand dollars. Again, financial stress: prayer; and some one put a banknote of five thousand dollars in Spurgeon's letter-box. The boys' section was erected first: building after building arose, one unit adjoining the other, until at the end of 1869 the boys' section was completed at a cost of fifty-one thousand dollars, all free of debt.

When at last Mrs. Hillyard's debentures "thawed out," all bills were paid, and her money became a permanent endowment.

Instances of this sort could be multiplied. Just one more: The year 1875 was very hard; funds low; then prayer. Spurgeon said plaintively in *The Sword and Trowel*, "Our boys persist in eating and wearing out clothes." In September a golden stream of fifty thousand dollars poured in, ten times more than was needed, so the balance was invested in permanent endowment funds.

The girls' section was projected in 1879. Gradually building after building was completed, and every claim met as it was due; also the annual current expense budget of twenty-five thousand dollars.

The Orphanage was within walking distance of the Tabernacle. It was a means of grace to see the five hundred children every Sunday morning in front of Spurgeon's pulpit, all unconscious of the fact that they were listening to the world's greatest preacher, but with love-lit faces watching him who was the best friend they ever knew.

Then there was the Pastors' College. It dates its beginning in the soul-surgery of Spurgeon, then twenty-one, upon a younger man, T. W. Medhurst, then twenty. Medhurst wanted to preach, and began with open-air meetings. Spurgeon saw how seriously Medhurst lacked elementary education, so he paid his tuition for two years at Bixley Heath, and concurrently tutored him in theology several hours each week. Then a church called Medhurst. Spurgeon suggested that the church pay the cost of Medhurst's education. They did. He offered the check to Medhurst, who vigorously refused it. Spurgeon said, "I gave that money to the Lord." He promptly used the check to take on a second student, E. J. Silverton, and the Pastors' College was under way.

In 1856 there were eight students; a few months later, twenty; then nearly one hundred. The primary aim was to provide simply elementary education for those whom God had evidently called to preach, but who were under disadvantage. The average course was two years. It never aimed to *make* men preachers, only to *help* those already called.

Once again Spurgeon said, "No debt." Rev. George Rogers (a Congregationalist) of Camberwell was the first tutor. The College met in Rogers' home; later in "certain dark, dungeon-like rooms in the basement of the Tabernacle; finally in their own beautiful building just back of the Tabernacle-free from debt!" But it was expensive to Spurgeon. His sermon sales netted him from three to four thousand dollars a year, which he poured into the College. Once he offered to sell "Punch's Coach" and "Peacock" (see XXI) when times were close. "Never!" thundered Rogers. They prayed-and the money came!

Further details about this great institution cannot be given here. By the time of Spurgeon's death nearly nine hundred men had been trained in it for the ministry; nine hundred men grounded in Puritan theology-because, he said, "Heresy in college means false doctrine in the churches." This ministerial host baptized tens of thousands of converts, erected scores of beautiful edifices, made a new day for the Baptist denomination, and, incidentally, listed such radiant alumni as Boreham of Australia.

"This treatment goes entirely around the building." To be sure the amazing sums of money necessary to finance these vast enterprises had their origin in the grace of God. Yet, God was able to show what he could do through a completely consecrated man.

Spurgeon's absolute unselfishness was the human clue to this riddle of high financing. When he found Christmas Evan's widow nearly starving, he privately supported her to the end of her days. Not a drop of mercenary blood in his veins! Like Russell H. Conwell, he made hundreds of thousands of dollars—and gave them all away. Redpaths offered him one hundred thousand dollars for one hundred lectures in America. Spurgeon responded, "No; I am a minister and have never lectured for money."

In May, 1879, the church gave him a purse of $32,380—no strings attached—in honor of his twenty-five years as pastor. He used it all to endow the Metropolitan Almshouses for elderly women. On Thursday evening, June 19, 1884, in honor of his fiftieth birthday, they gave him another purse, of $22,500—with very definite strings attached—this must be used for himself. He said, "What I have is best enjoyed by myself, personally, when I can use it in some way or other for the advantage of God's work. I cannot be debarred from this gratification." And he gave that money away.

The man's transparent honesty inspired all England with utter confidence. When any money was left his institutions which should have gone to worthy relatives, he gave it to them. Self-effacement under-girded self-realization. Over the vast institutions of Metropolitan Tabernacle one could write the sentence explanation: "Whosoever shall lose his life for my sake and the gospel's, the same shall save it."

Leaders of his stamp can finance any worthy project they feel led to sponsor. Mankind's sympathies run without reserve to such doers of "exploits." One of the tenderest stories of his life is of a poor woman who handed him five shillings. He said, "I don't want your money." "You must take it; I gave it to you because I got good from you." He asked, "Shall I give it to the College?" She answered, "I don't care about the College; I care about you." He replied, "You need it more than I do." She said, "Do you think your Lord and Master would have talked like that to the woman who broke the alabaster box over him? I worked extra to earn it, and I give it to you." Tears sprang to his eyes: "What *am* I to do with it?" And she said as she moved away from him, "Buy anything you like: I do not care what. Only mind, you must have it for yourself."

XX

BAGGAGEMEN

"Let us go into the house of the Lord," spoken by one hundred men in any city to those over whom they have influence, would raise a monster meeting. Many who would never come alone would come most willingly under the shadow of your company. You can *bring* multitudes whom you can never *send*. Therefore, brethren, to all whose ear and mind and heart you can command for such a purpose say, "Let us go—let us go together into the house of the Lord."—*Samuel Martin, "Gladness in the Prospect of Public Worship."*

I have often been amazed at the devotion of our brethren: I have told them many a time, that, if they would follow a broomstick as they have followed me, the work would succeed. —*C. H. S.*

Baggagemen

The very last time Spurgeon preached in Metropolitan Tabernacle was the Lord's Day morning of June 7, 1891. He appeared a broken man, "utterly weary in the Lord's work, but not of it"; prematurely old, though but fifty-six; his hair white, anguish lines in his face, so enfeebled that he supported himself with his right hand on the back of a chair. His sermon subject was "The Statute of David for Sharing the Spoil," the text 1 Samuel 30: 24, "As his share is that goeth down to the battle, so shall his share be that tarrieth by the baggage: they shall share alike." Throats were choked in the realization that the end was near. Yet the golden voice, gradually warmed and released by his glowing spirit, filled the Tabernacle with its mellow cadence.

It was a final love passage; one of the most beautiful tributes ever paid by a pastor to his people. The world, in speaking of the laborers at Metropolitan, might praise only a few; not so God; the humblest working girl, the poorest man, were equally praiseworthy in his sight. All the vast labors that had been accomplished had been wrought by God through the fidelity of people whom the world never knew about; men and women who prayed, and gave, and labored. The Son of God knew and remembered. It was life's largest worth while to serve a Captain like Him. His law was David's law; the baggagemen were as precious in His sight as the king. He concluded with those glorious words of praise for Christ as our leader, which I have recorded on the frontis of Chapter XXII.

It seems appropriate that his last sermon should have been what it was. However, there is no mystery in this, when we remember his texts were Spirit-given. Spurgeon knew, what this centennial year must never be allowed to forget, that his labors were underwritten by a race of self-effacing Britons whose chief business was the exaltation of Christ. George W. Truett likewise understands David's law of sharing the spoil. In pouring out his heart on this text to his people in the First Baptist Church of Dallas, he always says, "Brethren, it takes a great church to make a great preacher."

Spurgeon, mighty as he was, could never have moved his generation as he did without the thousands who humbly upheld his hands. None knew this better than he. Once, whimsically, he told a story of a French farmer whose crops were so large that he was accused of magic. The man immediately brought forth his stalwart sons and said, "Here is my magic!"

The materials selected for this chapter are frankly illustrative only. Thousands of noble men and women can never be mentioned. We specimen a few.

There was William Higgs the contractor who constructed Metropolitan Tabernacle; a business man of radiant Christian character, entirely self-effacing. Any pastor who has ever built a church knows how much of a blessing or of a curse the contractor may be. Concerning Higgs, Spurgeon said, "Eternity alone can reveal all the generous feeling and self-denying liberality evinced by Christian people in connection with the enterprise–to us, at any rate, so gigantic at the time that, apart from Divine aid, we could never have carried it through. One of the chief of our mercies was the fact that our beloved brother, William Higgs, was our builder, and treated us with unbounded liberality, throughout the whole affair." Higgs and his own baggagemen–his carpenters and masons–erected and gave an entire unit to the Orphanage. The New Park Street property was finally publicly auctioned off when it was found impractical to carry on a mission there. Higgs privately bid it in, sold it a few days later at a profit of $2,500, and then brought the entire sum and laid it on Spurgeon's desk as a gift to God. Small wonder that when Higgs died his widow was as a sister beloved to Spurgeon and Susannah.

Then there was the firm of Joseph Passmore and James Alabaster, Spurgeon's printers: "I am so attached to these friends that I have no wish to have any other publishers as long as I live; our business arrangements are such as Christian men would desire to make so that in all things God might be glorified." They stood by Spurgeon in the beginning with rare devotion. On Spurgeon's first Sunday in London young Passmore fell in love with him and insisted on walking home with him to the lodgings in Queen's Square. Shortly afterward he took a chance on the weekly publication of Spurgeon's sermons. It was hard to make ends meet, in the small pressroom, in the beginning, but Spurgeon's publications eventually made the firm wealthy. The letters between these three men are delicious bits of affection mingled with Simon-pure banter of the raciest sort. Even proof-sheets carry messages of good-natured comradery. Internal evidence convinces me that Passmore was the man who put his fortune on Spurgeon's bed when a great depression had overwhelmed him. Passmore was a heavy contributor to the College and to the Orphanage. The three men labored together for thirty-six years—and in the early nineties they all died within a very few months of each other.

Mention should be made of Spurgeon's only brother, the Rev. James A. Spurgeon. In 1868 he was called to be copastor. His was a rare soul, above jealousy. In accepting the call he wrote:

> "After my desire to glorify God, my sole object is to aid my brother, as he may desire me. It is in my heart by nature, and I am sure by grace, most cheerfully to give him that precedence which by birthright, talents, and position, is so justly his due. It is my privilege to be *first in love* to him."

Spurgeon's records are fragrant in love and appreciation of his brother's splendid labors. James died in 1898, after succeeding Charles as pastor of Metropolitan, and president of the Pastors' College.

We mention Mrs. Lavina Strickland Bartlett—and there were many of her kind. She taught a Bible school class of young women for sixteen years. The class averaged six hundred in attendance, one thousand of whom had joined the church when she died in 1875. Spurgeon said, "She aimed at soul-winning every time she met the class. Her talk never degenerated into story-telling, or quotations of poetry. She kept close to the cross, extolled her Saviour, pleaded with sinners to believe, and stirred up saints to holy living."

Concerning the rank and file, we quote Spurgeon's own words:

"Truly I may say, without the slightest flattery, that I never met with any people on the face of the earth who lived more truly up to this doctrine–that chosen of God, and loved by him with special love, they should do extraordinary things for him–than those among whom I have been so long and so happily associated. In service, they have gone beyond anything I could have asked; they have done it without request. Often I have brushed the tears from my eyes, when I have received from some of them offerings for the Lord's work which utterly surpassed all my ideas of giving."

Toward his deacons the full tide of his grateful love flowed out. They were a race of Amasiahs who offered themselves willingly unto God. Concerning them he wrote: "The church owes an immeasurable debt of gratitude to these men who study her interests day and night, contributing largely of their substance, care for her poor, cheer her ministers, and in every time of trouble as well as prosperity remain faithfully at their post. Our deacons are an honor to our faith, and we may style them, as the apostle did his brethren, 'the glory of Christ.'"

Such men as Carr, Mills, and the two Olneys have left records of peculiar love, energy, generosity and activity in God's service. They called Spurgeon "the Governor," and took the position that there must be only one captain in a ship. Their love for him was without measure. One became known as "Spurgeon's hunting dog," because he was always ready to pick up wounded birds–people impressed under the preaching of the Word.

What courage is put into the heart of a leader who receives such letters as this, one of scores written by his deacons: "And now beloved Pastor, we leave you with many prayers in the hands of your Father and our Father. May he have you in his safe-keeping, preserve you from lowness and depression of spirits, cheer you with the light of his countenance, strengthen and sustain you with his gracious Spirit, and in his own good time, bring you again to our beloved Tabernacle 'in the fulness of the blessing of the gospel of Christ.'"

Again, our inventory must end. But our contemporary Christianity, anxious to provide the world with more great churches–in God's sense of greatness–must remember that greatness begins with the rank and file. The name Spurgeon stands in high lights today because there were thousands of the same fair spirit as a certain one whom Spurgeon rebuked rather sharply, but who responded: "Well, that may be so; but I'll tell you what, sir, *I would die for you any day!*"

XXI
A Little Lower Than the Angels

Worse than a beast is man,
  Who after thine own image made at first,
Became a divel's sonne by sin.   And can
    A thing be more accurst?
Yet thou Thy greatest mercy hast
On this accursed creature cast.

Lo, man is made now even
  With the blest angels, yea, superiour farre,
Since Christ sat down at God's right hand in heaven,
    And God and man one are.
Thus all Thy mercy man inherits,
Though not the least of them he merits.
                    -Thomas Washbourne (1654).

Man is a little lower than the angels, and but a little, because time is short: and when that is over, saints are no longer lower than the angels. The margin reads, "A little *while* inferior to." All the dominion lost by sin is restored in Christ Jesus. Under our feet, therefore, we must keep the world: shun that base spirit which is content to let *anything* sway the empire of the immortal soul.-C. H. S.

A Little Lower Than the Angels

The Puritan concept of man-soul is not only enigmatic to the modern mind, it is *schrecklich*. The modern mind, in assured possession of which each generation preens itself—and dies!—understands Puritan divinity to put a degraded value upon human nature. Moderns, therefore, find their Puritan attitudes flavored with a mix of intolerable irritants—contempt, apprehension, injured pride and a roused inferiority complex; like Abigail's husband, though they are very great, they find no merit in David.

The chief tension between them and Puritan thinking lies in the use of the harmless-appearing word of Gladstone's, "unaided." The Puritans saw nothing but vileness in the unaided soul of man; otherwise, they considered him capable of boundless possibility. The modern mind is irritated by the implicates of unaided; it wishes the word stricken out entirely. The soul of man is capable of boundless possibilities. Right here, strangely enough, the chief tensions are appearing between the church and her present system of religious education; wise are those denominational leaders who awaken to the fact that the whole process has seeded to the cultural, and must now return to the spiritual, or stand for grubbing.

Actually, no more exalted view of human nature can be found than that of the Puritans. "If their names were not found in the registers of heralds, they were recorded in the Book of Life. Their diadems were crowns of glory which should never fade away. They esteemed themselves rich in a more precious treasure, and eloquent in a more sublime language. The very meanest man was a being to whose fate a mysterious and terrible importance belonged, who had been destined, before heaven and earth were created, to enjoy a felicity which should continue when heaven and earth should pass away."[1] *But*, these infinite possibilities are all involved in Christ's being formed within man; to this end Puritanism continually travailed. They regarded Nadab and Abihu's strange fire as nothing else than incitements of moral hopes, religious feelings and plans for personal improvements, that left out Jesus Christ.

This chapter aims to present the excellence of Spurgeon's manhood. But somehow in the writing of this book the Shadow of Spurgeon's Broad Brim has come over my spirit. The heart is out of me for the mere praising of any man, unless it be to observe that his virtues were really not of himself, but of the Christ that liveth in him. I seem to hear Spurgeon saying to George Needham—who proposed to write his life—"I am a poor subject; keep to the Lord Jesus." We shall keep to Jesus Christ, observing that the lovely fruits maturing in Spurgeon's heart were all of the Spirit, and, therefore, possible to the humblest of us.

A brief paragraph is sufficient upon the subject of Spurgeon's education. Too much time was given in

---

[1] Macaulay.

the past to working up a temperature over this question. His formal education appears to have been fully equivalent to that of an average American high school; but practically, his attainments were superb, a brilliant culture had by years of intense personal, extramural application. W. T. Stead once visited Westwood and in a friendly way tried Spurgeon's mental steel. Even in the matter of book reviewing the brilliance of Stead came off, confessedly, the worse for the encounter. Trained minds of the last century that were offended by Spurgeon's "lack of education" were all unhorsed by tumbling over the stumbling blocks of the vicious false premise that the only gates into the empire of culture are school gates. The educational processes through which Spurgeon passed were fully adequate. He was thoroughly equipped, though not a product of the schools.

When he came to London as a beardless youth he was becomingly slender, in his five foot six. But he rapidly achieved a notable embonpoint ("remarkably compact," thought Lorimer) that he carried to the end of his days. Like his grandfather, he had a large head—twenty-three inches around, to be precise. At about the age of thirty-five the clean-shaven face gave way to a Vandyke beard for "throat protection against London fog." Really, it helped to deepen the Shadow of the Broad Brim; for did not Puritans wear Vandykes? His eyes were the most striking facial feature: narrow-lidded, not quite matched, hazel brown. His whole soul looked out through those windows. They were never "slightly distended in dreaming," but always "intense observation in full repose." James Douglas said, "In conscious hours his eyes never slumbered." They were the body lights of an utterly fearless man whose soul was garrisoned in God, safe behind the barriers of a blameless life.

And his voice! It was a consistent unity, never slipping into a holy pulpit whine. George C. Lorimer, who reverenced voices, naturally gives the best description: "Marvelously sweet, resonant and tuneful; at one moment soft as a mother's lullaby, and at another ringing with all the clearness of a clarion calling cavalry troops to arms; rich, of great carrying quality, melodious, persuasive, sincere." Strangely enough, when a man becomes surrendered it is noted first in his voice. It was by the voices of Peter and John that the scribes took knowledge of them that they had been with Jesus. Christian oratory is naught else than the glad accommodation of nature to the purposes of a soul in love with Christ. H. L. Wayland asked, "What was that peculiar quality which made his voice audible long after we heard it in the outer ear?" Susannah said, "Even now in these lonely hours, I hear his dear voice *talking about Jesus.*"

Sheer mirth constantly bubbled up into those eyes and into that voice. Once criticized for causing laughter in his sermons, he said, "If you knew how much I suppress, you would forgive me." There was no great-man strut about him. Nearly all his correspondence was in his own handwriting. . . When he took up horseback riding to reduce, street gamins laughed at "the fat man on the nag"; Spurgeon laughed, too, and gave it up. He said, "The hobbyhorse in my grandfather's manse was the only one I ever enjoyed riding." The pure fun in life he never overlooked. A letter from someone who wrote, "Your book was read to my dear mother in her last illness, as long as she could bear it," brought a rollicking chuckle from the Westwood study. Think of the famous pastor of Metropolitan meeting the need of an unsuccessful old organ-grinder by himself taking over the organ while the uproarious hotel guests showered money out of the windows! When John Ruskin made catty remarks to him, Spurgeon's rebounds were models of harmless persiflage.

He could imitate any student in the Pastors' College, and did so when necessary for correction. He was sure six weeks is too long a vacation for a minister–See what happened when Moses was forty days on Sinai! Once when people in a congregation persisted in gawking, he burlesqued their interest in late-comers "to save the congregation the trouble of turning their heads"; and *did* it cure them! I have read many letters of his that fairly sparkle with affectionate banter. And he was a fountain of pure fun at all social occasions. Once at a wedding he said to the young couple, "I hope your wedded life will not be like the Church of England service, which begins with 'Dearly Beloved' and ends with 'amazement.'" At another time he said to the bride, "Remember Ephesians 5:23, 'The husband is head of the wife.' Don't try to be the head; but you be the neck, then you can turn the head whichever way you like." Theodore Cuyler used to relate how he and Spurgeon were laughing through Surrey woods one day, when suddenly Spurgeon said, "Come, Theodore, let us thank God for laughter." So closely related in his heart were God and joy.

American youngsters have a wise-crack, "If you can't take it, don't give it." Well, Spurgeon could surely take it; all his life he could laugh over jokes at his own expense. Jokes such as the story of a minister who prayed for him, when he was a boy preacher: "O Lord, our brother preached a good sermon; nothing very brilliant; but still likely to be useful." When he began to preach at Music Hall, an unknown censor mailed him every week a list of his mispronunciations and slips of speech. Spurgeon at one time had formed the habit—not unusual to public speakers—of overusing a phrase; for instance, "Nothing in my hand I bring." The anonymous censor wrote, "We are now sufficiently informed of the vacuity of your hand." Spurgeon said, "Ah, he was a valuable aid to progress."

This being a biography, not a panegyric, we have resolved neither to gloss over our subject's faults by way of making him a saint, nor to play up his peccadillos in order to ground a lark. So we must now face "a fissure from a division in character" where the Puritan got quite a little mixed. Against all worldliness he ran quite true to form: The stock market was "the devil's business"; the stage an "enemy to morals and religion"; he gave Joseph

Parker a thorough drubbing for his "view of religion that took him to a theater"; and then, alas! our hero *smoked a big black cigar!*

With Sidney Lanier, we grieve over failings of great men that bring them "quite a little lower than the angels." It is pathetic to read Spurgeon's British biographers as they try to explain away this uncouth habit. But he did smoke heavily throughout his life. Once he publicly tripped into saying that he smoked to the glory of God. He afterward half apologized for this bizarre statement, but made a sorry mess of it and achieved stultification. There is no defense. We submit none. Ninde weeps over Whitefield's casking rum to America and keeping slaves. Lanier's is the best way out; in a famous poem he lifts his weeping eyes from looking at the faults of his heroes to the Crystal Christ.

No better place appears in this biography for discussing certain pastoral relations. As to visitation, he could not of course even attempt the task; it was cared for by others, as were also wedding and funeral ceremonies. Nevertheless, Spurgeon did much calling, restricting his time to cases of genuine need. It should be remembered that he was pastor of the one church nearly forty years. A generation almost entirely new, like Israel entering Canaan, filled the Tabernacle at the close of his labors. Yet so marvelous was his memory of names and faces that he maintained vital contacts. He could look over the vast audience and remember who were present and absent.

One might expect a work that began with explosive

interest to cool down in a few years. It did. And here was his real test—to consolidate, invigorate and keep idealized a vast institution after romance had hardened into a task. He achieved it not by working a little more fervidly, but by keeping his idealism perennially fresh and vigorous. Or as George Santayana would put it, Spurgeon knew that "Fanaticism is redoubling your efforts when you've lost your aim."

I was surprised to find that Fullerton thought Spurgeon's sermons "mellowed down." This set me on a quest of comparisons of later with earlier sermons. Fullerton was obviously in error. Spurgeon's sermons did become more mature, less bombastic, but the altar-fire never decreased in the slightest (cf. "The Wedding Garment," 1888). The man was the same bright and shining light in 1892 that he was in 1854. And this explains why the Metropolitan Tabernacle did not begin degenerating at the fatal dead point.

One of the most adorable stories of his private life is told by Susannah. No "Henry" being then available for his country jaunts, he purchased an old horse—named, alas! "Peacock"—and a shabby old coach, to carry him out of the grinding unrest of London:

> "The vehicle was of so antiquated a pattern that it was immediately dubbed 'Punch's Coach,' and ever after bore that name. Its mirth-provoking aspect was increased when it was packed for a journey; there was an

arrangement behind that supported a board for luggage (trunk-rack) and added exceedingly to its grotesque appearance. I laughed afresh at every glimpse of it. I loved him so dearly that I even learned to appreciate 'Punch's Coach' for his sweet sake. As I write, and memories of the old days surge over my mind like the billows from a distant shore, I rejoice that his beaming, loving, satisfied face, as he started off on one of these country tours, is far more deeply impressed on my heart than the remembrance of his unsightly holiday caravan."

Susannah's statement, "He cared nothing for equipage," explains a curious phase of his life, carefully copied by his Jonathan, Dwight L. Moody; *he absolutely refused to be ordained:* Since no special gift could be bestowed, what was the sense of it? He preferred to remain unordained, unrecognized; and never discovered any peculiar loss he sustained thereby. Ordination prayers had a Babylonish sound in his ears: "Where is the scriptural warrant for such nonsense?" Early in New Park Street days the deacons pressed the matter. He responded, "I have decided objections. I am willing to submit, but it will be submission, nay, self-mortification." They dropped the matter, and to the end of life he was just "Mr. Spurgeon." Degrees were declined. "Reverend" he despised, and heavily crossed it off all proof sheets. "The cloth" was absurd to him: "The best canonicals in the world are thorough devotion to the Lord's work; this makes every garment a vestment." Eulogies were always painful; he was apt to break in with, "Not I, but Christ." He summed up his whole philosophy at this point in the words, "Christ opened a plain door and said, 'To follow me enter here.'"

Therefore he was the sworn enemy of pretense wherever found: "I have heard that more than four millions of money are squandered every year in funeral fopperies. The money buys or hires silk scarfs, brass nails, feathers for horses, kid gloves and gin for the mutes, and white satin and black cloth for the worms. It seems to me to be fine nonsense, more for the pride of the living than the honor of the dead, more for the profit of the undertaker than anyone else."

Like many another great leader, he found a sensitive spirit a marked detriment to sustained zeal; therefore he gave his soul an immunity bath in the following unique process:

"I have striven with all my might to attain the position of complete independence of all men. I have found, at times, if I have been much praised, and if my heart had given way a little, and I have taken notice of it and felt pleased, that the next time I was censored and abused I felt the censure and abuse more keenly, for the very fact that I accepted the commendation, rendered me more sensitive to the censure. So that I have tried, especially of late, to take no more notice of man's praise than his blame, but to rest simply upon this truth–I know I have a pure motive in what I attempt to do–to serve God with an eye single to his glory; and therefore it is not for me to take either praise or censure from man, but to stand independently upon the solid rock of right doing."

Love of nature, love of home and love of nation were cap-sheaf virtues in his humanity: "I love the glades and dells, the hills and vales, and have my fill of them." His pleasure was, "in the morning to startle the hare from her form, and in the evening, to talk with the countless stars." Sometimes, he visited London shops that he might take home to Susannah such objects as a chiming clock, or a dainty sewing-basket. Or being home at Westwood he delighted to walk or work in the garden with Dick the cat and the dogs Punch and Gyp frisking at his heels. And England—ah! "the sight of the eyes makes glad the heart!"

His crowning mental and spiritual grace was his utter humility. The origin of this virtue he traced to his conversion: "We might never have known such deep humility had not the Lord humbled us." Susannah, referring to the *Secret Diary*, says:

> "The words of the dear boy of sixteen are very touching when read in the light of his subsequent marvelous career. How marked is his humility, even though he must have felt the stirrings of wonderful powers. 'Forgive me, Lord,' he said in one place, 'if I have ever had high thoughts of myself.' . . Always intensely anxious to be kept from pride and self-glory. . . Notable is this sentence in the Diary,

'Make me thy faithful servant, O my God; may I honor thee in my day and generation, and be consecrated forever to thy service.'"

He pleaded with God, in the Diary, to keep him mindful that he had nothing that he did not receive. This deep humility grew with each passing year, and caused one who at first was rather unfriendly to say, "So far from self-esteem growing with his extending fame, he appears to be more humble and more subdued than when he first burst on our astonished gaze." To the end of his days, his whole being was subordinated to one loving motive, that in all things He might have the preeminence!

How altogether exalted the manhood of this Puritan! The memory of his Christ-centered heart, the vivacity of his conversation, the beauty of his love and self-effacement have made thousands who knew him, mindful how altogether like unto the angels are those who consort with Christ. "Thou madest him a little lower than the angels."

XXII

CHRISTOCENTRIC

Spurgeon's First Words in the Metropolitan Tabernacle, Monday afternoon, March 25, 1861 (per Schindler):

"I shall scarcely attempt a sermon, . . but truths from which future sermons will be made . . . bullion rather than coin. In the days of Paul, the sum and substance of theology was JESUS CHRIST. I would propose that the subject of the ministry of this house, as long as this platform shall stand, shall be the person of JESUS CHRIST. I am not ashamed to vow myself a Calvinist. . . I do not hesitate to take the name of Baptist. . . But if I am asked what is my creed, I must reply, 'It is JESUS CHRIST' . . . CHRIST JESUS, who is the sum and substance of the gospel, the incarnation of every previous truth, the all glorious embodiment of the way, the truth, and the life!"

Spurgeon's Last Words in the Metropolitan Tabernacle, Sunday morning, June 7, 1891 (per Susannah):

"Jesus Christ is the most magnanimous of Captains. There never was His like among the choicest of princes. The heaviest end of the Cross lies ever on His shoulders. If there is anything that is gracious, generous, kind, and tender, yea lavish and superabundant in love, you always find it in Him! His service is life, peace, joy. Oh, that you would enter it at once! *God help you to enlist under the banner of Jesus Christ!*"

CHRISTOCENTRIC

Fairbairn in his day came nearly enforcing the rewriting of Christian theology by that which was implicate in his term, "Christocentric." It was a new idea to Fairbairn's generation, but it is the most ancient approach of the church. In the first few years during and after the apostolic era *Christ Jesus* was preached; then, insensibly, the church went centrifugal. It began to evaluate Christianity in terms of doctrines, ceremonials, offices, moral derivatives, social applications and topical chit-chat. The church at last became thoroughly lost in her own synthetic orbits. She showed no exception to the general tendency of man to get farther and farther away from the living personality of Christ to a frame of finespun doctrines about him; and at last to a denatured faith which justified its keeping the label "Christian" by tossing Jesus a compliment now and then.

The Christocentric mind is one that repudiates any kind of thinking, choosing, planning, emotion, action, which does not have at its center the living Person Jesus. Practically every age has produced these centripetal Christians, men with a heated impatience toward the cold tweedledums and dees of ethical preaching; and a sharp aversion to pulpit connoisseurs in word tapestry. They yearn for Jesus. They demand of themselves what they expect in every Christian, the evidence that all actions begin and end with the warm, sweet Presence, living yet. The

Puritans were Christocentric men. They rejected with contempt the ceremonious homage which other sects substituted for the pure worship of the soul; they aspired to gaze full on his intolerable brightness, and to commune with him face to face. Like sturdy old Fleetwood, the only bitterness of soul they knew was when Jesus hid his face from them. On every other subject they were tranquil. They had their smiles and their tears, their raptures and their sorrows, but they were all associated with the Young Son of God, not the affairs of a world that was to them but a painted picture.

There have been many Puritans since the days of the Puritans, though often unaware of it. Flaming Sam, of Gramercy Park, certainly has the Shadow on his face. Read his comments on Bishop Fiske's *Confession of a Puzzled Parson.* Sam could answer the enigma of a decadent church:

> "The careless organization; the unenthusiastic service; the listless preaching; the vague feeling of unreality about it all; how little it does for those who come; how little attraction it holds for those who do not; the restlessness of the ministers, coming out in desire to change parishes, or communions, or callings . . . these things are not causes, they are symptoms. The first cause is a defective experience of Jesus Christ in the clergy."

Yes, many Puritans since! Listen to E. Stanley Jones for an hour, and then it would seem natural to behold him slip on his overcoat and reach for a

Broad Brim. The strange power of this apostle from India is naught else than his Christocentric faith, even though his Friend be mainly the Christ of the Mount. Strange power all such men exert on their contemporaries! "They go through the world, like Sir Artegal's iron man, Talus, with his flail, having neither part nor lot with human infirmities, insensible to fatigue, to pleasure, and to pain, not to be pierced by any weapon, not to be withstood by any barrier!"

In these closing chapters, we are tracing to its finality the hidings of Spurgeon's genius—*the Son of God was everything to him!* Theology was evermore a poor second: "I bind myself precisely to no form of doctrine. I love those five points (of Calvin) as being the angles of the gospel, but, then, I love the Center between the angles better still." The deep reality of Jesus dyed his whole life. When I began to read his early letters, letters which he never dreamed would be read by others after his death, and therefore most natural, I confess that shame mounted my cheeks to find how real Jesus was to this British boy, how he adored him; and to remember how late in life it was before my own defective experience was remedied. If Spurgeon wrote to his mother it was always, "Kiss the little ones (his brother and sisters) and give them my love. May they learn of Jesus." A lad with a sweetheart never referred to her in his correspondence with more evident pride and affection than he did to Christ.

In the *Little Secret Diary*, we find such rare Canticles as this:

"*April 12,1850.* Earthly things have engaged too much of my thoughts this day. I have not been able to fix my attention entirely upon my Saviour. I would be ever with Thee, O my spotless, fairest Beloved! Daily meet me, for Thy embrace is Heaven; sanctify me, prepare me, help me to bring forth fruit and to be Thine forever! 'Tell me, O Thou whom my soul loveth, where Thou feedest, where Thou makest thy flock to rest at noon!'"

Spurgeon's power in prayer and his personal prayer life was perhaps the most prominent aspect of this many-sided man. Through the years in which I have had opportunity to meet people who heard him in the Metropolitan Tabernacle, I have been amazed at the number who considered the pulpit-prayers to be the most memorable part of the services. There was aged Deacon Samuel Gillette, retired in the sunny deserts of Arizona, who, so often as I pressed him for details of Spurgeon's voice, his preaching, would appear confused, but would always rally: "Ah, you should have heard him pray!" Not much fuller information came from Prof. J. P. Fruit; but I heard him say a score of times in English classes, "When Spurgeon prayed, it seemed as if Jesus stood right beside him."

This deep devotion came upon Spurgeon at his conversion. Here is a typical section from his letters home: "19th Sept. '50. Dear Father: . . We have a prayer-meeting at seven in the morning. . . How soon would the lamps go out did not our mighty Lord supply fresh oil!" Here is a section from *Lectures to My Students:* "Live near to God . . . if your zeal grows dull, you will not pray well in the pulpit. . . worse in the family . . . worst in the study alone. When your soul becomes lean, your hearers, without knowing how or why, will find that your prayers in public have little savor in them." Again: "If true to his Master, the preacher becomes distinguished for his prayerfulness." Susannah said, "The dear preacher greatly valued the season of devotion in the half-hour before time for commencing the service." This type of private devotion was essentially a waiting for direction; he seldom even wrote a letter without raising his heart to Christ for guidance.

Concerning those amazing public prayers, Pike says, "You feel instinctively when he prays that here is a man strong enough to bear up on his anointed hands the prayers of a host—the grandest idea that ever entered into the thoughts of a priesthood between God and men." Too bad those prayers were not preserved! But Spurgeon flatly forbade that his public prayers should be printed. Fortunately a few samples may be gleaned from old articles, books, etc. Here is one from Justin D. Fulton's *Spurgeon Our Ally.* He described a prayer-service in Metropolitan Tabernacle that dragged wretchedly. Finally Deacon Olney said to Spurgeon, "*You* had better take the meeting."

Spurgeon prayed: "O God, here is the devil doing his best to break up this prayer-meeting. I hear him say, 'The church is dead, faith is dying out.' I hear him, Lord, claiming that the people are satisfied with great congregations and that they are letting go of the right hand of the Lord Jesus. It is a lie, O God! We trust in Thee, Jesus! (On he went, praising Christ. 'Amens' began to roll forth.) Come, Lord Jesus, lift us out of ourselves and into Thee!"

Fulton concludes: "'Amen!' was our united shout, and the work was done. The tide of redeeming love came in . . . we were out on the ocean of God's love, sailing." From the very outset, prayer was consistently Spurgeon's reliance for the empowerment of the church. His explanation of New Park Street Chapel's clinging to life in her destitute days was: "There were in the midst of the church a few who never ceased to pray for a gracious revival." And here is a bit of inside history to which reference seems never to have been made. There was an appreciable interval *after* Spurgeon took the pastorate before the manifestation of power began. Pentecost in New Park Street Chapel started in prayer. I quote his own words:

"There was a mere handful to whom I first preached. (Not the first sermon, but the first weeks.) Yet, I can never forget how earnestly they prayed. Sometimes they seemed to plead as though they could really see the Angel of the Covenant present with them, and as if they must have a blessing from Him.

"More than once we were all so awestruck with the solemnity of the meeting that we sat silent for some moments while the Lord's power appeared to overshadow us; and all I could do on such occasions was to pronounce the Benediction and say, 'Dear

Friends, we have had the Spirit of God here very manifestly tonight; let us go home and take care not to lose his gracious influences.'

"Then came down the blessing; the house was filled with hearers, and many souls were saved!"

With him it was Jesus always and Jesus only. Susannah as a young wife wrote of their early travels: "We had family prayer, whether we lodged in some rough inn on the mountains, or in the luxurious rooms of a palatial hotel in a city; and the blessed 'abiding in Christ,' of which many of us say, 'It is high, I cannot attain unto it,' was to him the natural atmosphere of his soul; he lived and breathed in Him."

It is worth while to read Spurgeon's account of his woodland jaunts, not only for the high descriptive beauty, but to get the cool, silver shock of the Living Water flowing throughout the pages: "We have roamed the woods for two hours, and have never seen a soul. Birds, rabbits, ants and spiders have been our only company, save the One with whom we hold sweet converse. . ." And it makes drama of the highest order to read how once he climbed to the very top of the Coliseum, looked at the arena where Christians died for the faith, and then began to sing, "*I'm* not shamed to own my Lord." Never mind American tourists who looked up and kidded him; on he went, like one of those "Happy-Of-Such-Children," singing, "Am I a Soldier of the Cross?" and "Ashamed of Jesus."

The very richness and vastness of the incidents showing Spurgeon's Christocentric life are embarrassing. Three more, selected at random, sample the run of the rest. William H. Geistweit, broken from hard work in an early pastorate in New Jersey, spent a winter in Mentone. He met Spurgeon there. One day he was walking in the street when the great preacher espied him from his carriage. "He hailed me," wrote Geistweit, "and when I approached him, held out his left hand and said cheerily, 'Oh, you are worth five shillings a pound more than when I saw you last,' and letting his voice fall to a tone of deep earnestness, he added, 'Spend it all for the Lord.'" W. Y. Fullerton wrote: "His language at the Lord's Table would have been considered extravagant if one did not know how perfectly real it was. 'Well-Beloved' was the name he oftenest used for his Saviour. From praying, he would take to talking, and from talking he would stand and soliloquize about his Lord, and the audience felt he was simply enraptured with him."

The author of this book confesses he was unexpectedly moved to tears in reading one of Spurgeon's travelog lectures. It was engrossingly written. Within seven lines of the end he suddenly finished with this startling peroration: "One more remark and I am done. If you cannot travel, remember that our Lord Jesus Christ is more glorious than all else that you could ever see. Get a view of Christ and you have seen more than mountains and cascades and valleys and seas can ever show you. Earth may give its beauty, and stars their brightness, but all these put together can never rival Him."

No wonder hackneyed texts sprang to life under

his touch. Christ was the secret of his power. Lord Shaftesbury, whom Hodder immortalized, wrote to Spurgeon under date of May 14, 1881: "Signal as are the talents that God has bestowed upon you, they would without preaching Christ in all his majestic simplicity have availed you nothing to comfort and instruct the hearts of thousands."

His Christocentric life was never a studied part, never an actor's gesture. It was real; every atom of his manhood, all there was in him and of him, belonged to the Son of God. When he lay dying in Mentone, Susannah lingered beside him. She wept softly as he lay for hours unconscious. She smiled bravely through her tears when for short intervals he spoke with her. Out of her grief she wrote: "Perhaps of greatest price among the precious things which this little book (the *Secret Diary*) reveals, is the beloved author's personal and intense love for the Lord Jesus. He lived in His embrace; like the apostle John, his head leaned on Jesu's bosom ("Jesu" was his private and intimate term of endearment for his Lord). The endearing terms, used in the Diary and never discontinued, were not empty words."

When the end drew near, he whispered, "Susie." She bent close to listen, clasped his hand in hers and said, "Yes, dear Tirshatha." And he murmured—the last words before he saw Him face to face—"Oh, wifie, I have had such a blessed time with my Lord."

Tirshatha and the Puritans
("His Latest and Best," Susannah)

XXIII

Pilgrim Passes Over

Boys, when they see a bear, a lion, or a wolf dead in the street will pull off their hair, insult over them, and deal with them as they please; they will trample upon their bodies, and do that unto them being *dead*, which they durst not in the least venture upon whilst they are *alive*. Such a thing is Death, a furious beast, a ramping lion, a devouring wolf, the *hellus generis humani* (eater up of mankind). Yet Christ has laid him at his length, hath been the death of death, so that God's children have played upon him, scorned and derided him, by the faith they had in the life of Christ, who hath subdued him.—*Martin Day (1660).*

The dying saint is not in a flurry; he keeps to his old pace—he walks. The last days of a Christian are the most peaceful of his whole career; many a saint has reaped more joy and knowledge when he came to die than ever he knew while he lived. *When there is a shadow there must be a light somewhere.* The light of Jesus shining upon death throws a shadow across our path; let us therefore rejoice for the Light beyond!—*C. H. S.*

Pilgrim Passes Over

The shadows of the old year are growing long the December night the writing of this biography comes to a close. In a few days the world will lie in the soft radiance of Christmas. It does not seem possible that more than a year has passed since I began to gather sheaves–from the vast memorabilia–for a new Life of Charles Haddon Spurgeon. What an exacting task it has been! Yet by reason of the deeper fellowship with the Son of God this study has yielded I would attempt it again, were it ten times as hard. Never has the name Emmanuel meant so much to me as tonight, in this great city by the Golden Gate, radiant with Christmas decorations. It seems fitting that I should chronicle Spurgeon's coronation while the Star of Bethlehem is again lighting the world.

The closing six months of his life may be swiftly sketched. On June 7, 1891, he preached his last sermon in Metropolitan. A few hours later, with almost premonitory feelings, he limped through the streets of Stambourne, to view and photograph precious childhood scenes. Then he hurried to Westwood, a very sick man. Overpowering headaches came on: "I had to hurry home, go to that chamber where for three months I suffered beyond measure." The world now seemed to sense the end, and to appreciate how faithfully this David had served his generation, by the will of God. Telegrams, cablegrams, letters, resolutions of sympathy, poured in from all over the world to Susannah.

For the most of the time until October, the patient was bedfast in the master chamber on the second story of Westwood, his condition being a long and wearisome alternating of hopeful advances and disappointing relapses. To escape the approaching London winter, the doctor's staff decided it was wise to start him off to Mentone at once. The family physician told Susannah she was now well enough to go with him. Tears of joy flooded her eyes. It was her first journey with him in years. She quickly made her way to his bedside and whispered, "O Tirshatha, I go with you!" She later wrote: "Ah, it was a tender token of the Lord's loving kindness, that we were for once permitted to travel to Mentone together, and to spend there three months of perfect happiness, before the sorrowful separation."

Mentone days were unusually bright that fall, but the radiance did not exceed the joy of Susannah and Tirshatha, in their long visits together, and in their short drives on the Boulevard Victoria.

Every scene of Mentone had become precious to Spurgeon's heart; had he not made nearly twenty annual visits to this Mediterranean Paradise? had he not watched it in that time grow from a little village to a fair-sized town? and did he not know every blessed tradition and golden story about its charming history? And thus in these happy, farewell days the voice of Tirshatha went on and on, telling Susannah of events in the past when he had come alone. It now seemed as sweet to her to hear him tell it as if she, escaping her long sickness, could have accompanied him each year. "So the Dear Father heals even the memory of tribulation."

Southern France seemed set for their peculiar delight. Never did the olive groves bear such powdered silver sheen on the under side of their dark green leaves. The waters of the Mediterranean were lobelia-blue throughout the crisp fall days; and the vast Alpine mountains, that come down almost to the shore, were masses of tender pastel shades. The coral tiles and white walls of homes and public buildings, in their winding streets, looked like dreams of Bethlehem beneath the azure skies. Susannah counted over as her rosary of memory every precious hour of these last days together; waiting, waiting at Westwood, while Tirshatha was at home with God.

On the evening of Sunday, January 17, 1892, Spurgeon attended his last service, held privately in his sitting-room at the hotel. On the afternoon of January 20, gout swellings appeared in his right hand, and later in the day other serious symptoms: he had to retire to the bed from which he never again rose. On Saturday, January 23, he said to his secretary, "My work is done." Tuesday, January 26, he sent a loving cable to the members of Metropolitan. On Wednesday, January 27, he became totally unconscious, and remained so until five minutes past eleven, Sunday night, January 31, 1892, when ——

Let Susannah, in her tears, in the delicate beauty of her own language, tell: "Like his namesake, Mr. Valiant-for-truth, he passed over, and all the trumpets sounded for him on the other side." Then she fell to her knees and said: "Blessed Lord Jesus, I thank Thee for the precious treasure so long lent me; now, be pleased to give me strength and guidance for all the future."

W. Y. Fullerton supplies valuable details of the funeral services. Sixty thousand persons participated. On the casket there was a Bible, open at the text, "Look unto me all ye ends of the earth!" Fullerton adds the pathetic touch, at the end of his book: "The people at home were anticipating his return; they were building a lift at the rear of the Tabernacle to save him the exertion of walking up the stairs. But others were waiting for him, too, in the unclouded country; and thither he went."

The lights of his centennial year are beginning to glow. Meanwhile the world is at Dreadful Crossroads. But somehow, in the light of the life of Charles Haddon Spurgeon, I feel that it doesn't matter. We are also at the portals of a great spiritual awakening. The love of God shall cover the earth afresh, and the ghastly spectres of crime, sin and unbelief fade away in the light of his face. All the Son of God requires to bring in a better age is that we who bear his sign shall be utterly disciplined to his will, our souls revised, invaded and heated by his presence; our hearts reaffirming the words of another Valiant of the Broad Brim, John Owen:

"From the crown of my head to the soles of my feet, there is not one drop of blood but that I would gladly shed for my Lord, Jesus Christ!"

Biographical Dates

Born, Kelveden, Essex, June 19, 1834.

Moves to Colchester, April 18, 1835.

Lives with grandparents, August, 1835, to August, 1841.

Richard Knill incident, summer, 1844.

School at New Market, August, 1849.

Born again, January 6, 1850.

Baptized (mother's birthday), May 3, 1850.

Enters Leedings' School, Cambridge, June 20, 1850.

Joins St. Andrew's Baptist Church, Cambridge, by letter, October 2, 1850.

First sermon, spring of 1851.

First sermon at Waterbeach, October, 1851.

Receives invitation to preach at New Park Street Baptist Church, November, 1853.

First sermon in New Park Street, December 18, 1853.

Called to New Park Street, April 19, 1854.

Accepts call, April 28, 1854.

Preaches in Exeter Hall, February-March, 1855.

Married to Susannah Thompson, January 8, 1856.

Paris honeymoon, January, 1856.

Twin sons born, September 20, 1856.

Surrey Hall Tragedy, October, 1856.

Morning services Surrey Hall, November, 1856, to December, 1859.

Tabernacle Building Committee appointed, June, 1856.

Preaches at Crystal Palace, October 7, 1857.

Moves to New Kent Road, fall of 1857.

Site of Tabernacle purchased, December 13, 1858.

Corner-stone of Tabernacle laid, August 16, 1859.
First meeting in Tabernacle, August 21, 1860.
Tabernacle opened, March 18, 1861.
Site for orphanage purchased, January, 1867.
Preaches in Agricultural Hall, March-April, 1867.
Foundation of orphanage laid, August 9, 1867.
Wife becomes helpless invalid, 1868.
Helensburgh house built, summer, 1869.
Twin sons baptized, September 21, 1874.
Moves to Westwood, summer, 1880.
Last sermon, June 7, 1891.
Died, January 31, 1892.
Buried at Norwood, February 11, 1892.